AR.

A Purbeck Parish in Peace and War

Terence Davis

Arne Church.

DORSET PUBLISHING COMPANY
NATIONAL SCHOOL, NORTH STREET
WINCANTON, SOMERSET BA9 9AT

First published MM by Dorset Publishing Company from the National School, North Street, Wincanton, Somerset BA9 9AT (telephone 01-963-32583)

Typeset by Julie Green and printed by F.W.B. Printing at Bennetts Mead, Southgate Road, Wincanton, Somerset BA9 9EB (telephone 01-963-33755)

Distributed by Halsgrove from Lower Moor Way, Tiverton, Devon EX16 6SS (telephone 01-884-243-242)

International standard book number [ISBN] 0 948699 74 4

Contents

*Arne's speciality species, in a delightful drawing of a Dartford Warbler,
perched on a sprig of furze, from J. C. Mansel-Pleydell's* Birds of Dorsetshire, *1888.
He laments that 'it is doubtful whether we shall any longer see our heaths
enlivened by this active little bird'. Thankfully, due to a succession of mild winters,
he has been proved quite wrong.*

Map of the Arne Peninsula

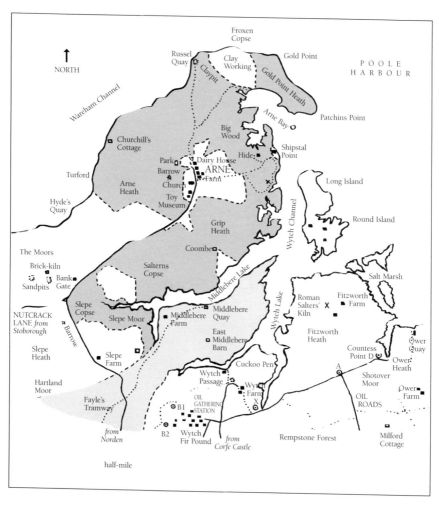

NORTH

POOLE HARBOUR

Froxen Copse
Russel Quay
Clay Working
Gold Point
Claypit
Gold Point Heath
Wareham Channel
Arne Bay
Patchins Point
Churchill's Cottage
Big Wood
Hide
Shipstal Point
Park Barrow
Dairy House
ARNE Farm
Turford
Arne Heath
Church
Toy Museum
Long Island
Hyde's Quay
Wytch Channel
Grip Heath
Round Island
Coombe
The Moors
Salterns Copse
Salt Marsh
Brick-kiln
Bank Gate
Sandpits
Middlebere Lake
Roman Salters' Kiln
Fitzworth Farm
Slepe Copse
Slepe Moor
Middlebere Farm
Middlebere Quay
Wytch Lake
Fitzworth Heath
Ower Quay
NUTCRACK LANE from Stoborough
Barrow
East Middlebere Barn
Countess Point D
Ower Heath
Slepe Heath
Slepe Farm
Cuckoo Pen
Shotover Moor
Ower Farm
Hartland Moor
Wytch Passage
Wytch Farm
OIL ROADS
Ower Farm
Fayle's Tramway
OIL GATHERING STATION
B1
from Norden
B2
Wytch Fir Pound
from Corfe Castle
Rempstone Forest
Milford Cottage

half-mile

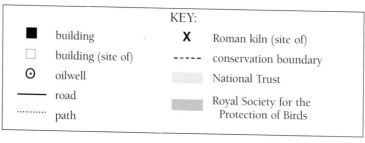

KEY:

■	building	
□	building (site of)	
⊙	oilwell	
—	road	
....	path	

X   Roman kiln (site of)

-----   conservation boundary

    National Trust

    Royal Society for the Protection of Birds

Phyl Marsh aged 21.
This picture was taken by the Wimborne photographer Stan James who was scoutmaster of the 1st Wimborne Scouts. They came regularly to Arne to camp.

Typical heathland at Arne, with a bomb crater in the foreground now serving as a pond for dragonflies, and a distant glimpse of the former Hamworthy Power Station. Seen from beside Arne Bay with Patchins Point in the middle distance.

A Romano-British pottery kiln found in 1952 in a field to the north of Nutcrack Lane at Ridge.

Author's Note

This is Phyl Marsh's book. She has been unstinting in giving her memories of a period now long vanished. Without them there would have been no book on Arne. She has also given freely of her time, to collect for me a variety of photographic material, to introduce me to a large number of other people who gladly helped in adding to what I knew, and to take me round the area, which added a new dimension to my knowledge.

To Dorrie Churchill, the late Florence Coombes, her son, Dennis, and to the late Reg Smith and his sister, Nancy, I owe a tremendous debt.

I must also thank all those who wrote in answer to my newspaper request for information, and especially to Don Gilbert, Jim Hearmon, and to many others.

I am also indebted to the staff at The Dorset County Record Office for the use of the records within their care, and to Poole Borough Library staff.

To all who have contributed in any way, I say "Thank you!".

Although this book is really concerned with the period 1850 to 1942, Arne, Purbeck's cul-de-sac community, is much older. No one actually knows from which source county historian and Wareham rector John Hutchins drew his information that in the time of Richard II the village belonged to Shaftesbury Abbey and that there were 24 tenants, or, perhaps, more correctly, there were 24 families living there. However, the little church is around two hundred years older, dating from about 1200. This means that there was a definite settlement there then large enough to warrant a church of its own.

Anton Fagersten in 1933 noted that the name "Arne" first occurs in a document dated 1285, and, according to A. D. Mills, in 1977, this is still its first accepted earliest documentary reference. However, archaeological evidence has pushed human activity in the area back very much further. In Roman times, people were extracting salt in the area north of the present Bank Gate Cottages, and before them, the people of the Bronze Age built two burial mounds [round barrows] on Arne Hill. All this suggests that there must have been men, women and children living in the area long before the little church was built about 1200, though it must be admitted that William the Conqueror's Domesday Book investigators of 1085-88 did not mention Arne, which is very puzzling if there was a village there then.

Evidence from Arne's history between 1200 and the eighteenth century is very limited, although Barbara Kerr has considerably extended our knowledge of land holding in the eighteenth and nineteenth centuries. It is largely the period after this date that this book is dealing with, after John Scott, the second Earl of Eldon [1803-1854] had acquired Arne from the

Filliters, who were lawyers in the nearby town of Wareham. From now on, the area was administered from Encombe, the Scott's headquarters in the Golden Bowl beyond Kingston.

They were a remarkable family, for the second Earl's grandfather had only been a prominent merchant in Newcastle on Tyne in the eighteenth century, but one of his sons, John [born in 1751], had chosen law as his profession and had become so outstanding that he had been created a baron for this in 1799, and two years later Lord Chancellor, a post he held under a succession of Prime Ministers until his resignation in 1827. He has gone down in history as a die-hard reactionary Tory, against all reform, and an enemy of parliamentary democracy, a reputation drawn up by the leading Whigs of his day and preserved and continued by a succession of Liberal historians ever since.

However, it is the third Earl, another John, whom older people remember as the owner of the Encombe estate; a "dear old soul," according to Phyl Marsh, ". . . rough and ready. He used to ride a bicycle. My father taught him to shoot." By the 1920s, he was well into his seventies. He died in 1926 and was succeeded as Earl by his son, another John, then in this middle twenties, but the Encombe estate went to his brother, Sir Ernest Scott, then in his middle fifties.

Sources

A. Fagersten, *The Place-Names of Dorset*, 1933, pp. 129-130.
A. Mills, *The Place-Names of Dorset*, vol. 1, 1977, pp. 71-73.
Reverend J. Hutchins, *The History and Antiquities of the County of Dorset*, 2nd Edition, ed. R. Gough and J. Nichols, 1796-1815; 3rd Edition, ed. W. Shipp and J. Hodson, 1861-1870.
B. Kerr, *Bound To The Soil*, 1968, pp. 27-29.
Burke's Peerage for 1931; and for 1949.

The Earl of Eldon —
rode his bike to Arne.

Introduction

Arne as "the hiding place" was how Canon Blackett the one time rector of Wareham once described the meaning of village's name in one of his sermons. He may have been wrong in his derivation, but he was certainly right about its geography. A modern postcard calls it "the secret place", and it is! Not many of the cars that go hurtling along the by-pass to Corfe Castle and Swanage turn off at Stoborough and take the three mile winding road eastward across the heath towards the harbour to Arne, but more visitors now come each year than used to in the 1950s. The Royal Society for the Protection of Birds' sanctuary has placed the village more firmly on the map, while the toy museum draws other visitors, as does the church of St. Nicholas, a little gem of a building. Others come to wander down the dusty track, as people have done for centuries, though the twentieth century visitor is more likely to play on the beach or in the water, rather than to fish, as people in the past would have done.

Once down at Shipstal, the immediate scene has changed little over the centuries. It can still seem deserted and isolated. The fishermen's boats, it is true, have been replaced by more luxurious craft, yachts, motorboats, and such like.

Shut your eyes and listen to the sounds, to the birds' cries and the gently lapping waves on the shore, and you could be back in the last century or earlier, but open them and look at Hamworthy and Poole, and the twentieth century hits you squarely in the eyes with its white modernity.

Today most of the houses are at Arne, though there are a few cottages at Bank Gate, at Shipstal and at Slepe, but before the Second World War it would have been very different, with more cottages both at Arne and elsewhere in the area.

A journey from Stoborough would then have involved a bumpy ride along the stoney road, very dusty in summer. Past Ridge, which was developing quickly in the interwar years, and across the railway line that brought clay from the pits at Furzebrook down to the river at Ridge, the traveller reached the open heathland, all purple, brown and yellow. To the left on The Moors, young heifers could be seen grazing on the rough pastures that were intersected by several deep ditches, which were often marked along their length with masses of water lilies.

Further on, Duckbog Lane went off to the right. Some way along this towards Corfe was a large pond, which gave it its name. Not far from its junction with the main road between Wareham and Corfe was the Isolation Hospital for Wareham and the Purbeck area.

On the map, this is called Soldiers Road, but Phyl Marsh has always known it as Duckbog Lane. Its alternative name may date from the First World War, when many soldiers spent many weeks training in this area.

Nearly a mile beyond Duckbog Lane back on the way to Arne, again on the right, another track led down to the hamlet of Slepe [pronounced "Slip" by the locals]. This is now little more than just the farm. Then, it was a scattered group of many cottages.

Just beyond this turning stood, and still stand, Bank Gate Cottages, a terrace of three, which had been built about 1890. They are first mentioned in the 1891 Census. Here in the 1930s lived Bill Diamond, who worked on the estate, and his daughter. Next door came Reg Smith and his wife, and in the third of the terrace lived Alfie Lines and his wife, Ivy. They worked as gardener and cook up at Arne House. Nearly opposite Bank Gate, a decoy was built during the Second World War, which was to play an important part in the history of the village.

A little further on was a white gate that always stood open. It marked the official beginning of the hamlet. It was here that there was a platform on the roadside for the milk churns. From here, the track to Arne went up Goddles

Frederick Charles Loseby who was keeper at Arne from 1930 to about February 1934. Information from his son, Eric.

Cyril Ford took over as keeper from Frederick Loseby and was in post until the wartime evacuation.

12

Keeper's Cottage is now the Toy Museum.

Knap, with Salterns Wood on the right, where a German plane was brought down during the war, and three of the soldiers from the local camp were stationed for three or four days to guard it.

The road now undulated gently up and down over Little Chemist Hill, but today the traveller is hardly likely to notice any climb. Successive repairs have ironed out its little hump. Next came Chemist Hill. The rise here is slightly more noticeable today, but it is very gentle. The hill was so called apparently because the chemist used to come as far as this hill, and would not come any further. Anyone who had toothache came to him and he would take it out on the spot.

A little further on along the road, a track went off on the right down through the wood to Coombe and the shore. Here in the nineteenth century was a small cluster of cottages, but when the last tenants, the Fianders, moved out in the 1930s, the buildings began to decay and crumble, and have now disappeared.

Back again on the main road from Stoborough, and beyond the Coombe turning stood a large building on the left, set back from the road. This today is the Toy Museum, but it occupies the one-time kennels for Lord Eldon's dogs. They were looked after by a keeper, who lived in the house adjoining.

Opposite the museum today is the visitors' car-park, created by the Royal Society for the Protection of Birds, which now controls much of the Arne Peninsula. Before the Second World War, the site was the tennis court belonging to Arne House.

Carter Roberts's Cottage and farm outbuildings.

From here, then as now, the road goes up a short rise and is set deep between banks which rise sheer on each side, and is overhung with trees. It is appropriately known as Deep Street. At night, the place would seem especially dark, and many villagers hated walking along it then. In the 1930s Phyl Candy was one of these.

High above on the bank on the left hand side was Arne House, leased before the Second World War to the Wood family from London as a summer holiday home. At the top of Deep Street, the main village came into sight, with the small church, grey stone and ancient, on the left, and the old schoolhouse on the right.

In front, and blocking the way stood Arne Farm, the solid Victorian home of the Candys, with its large yard behind it. The house was severely damaged in the war and was pulled down in the 1950s. A new house was then built a little back from the old site. Behind this was a double fronted, brick and tiled cottage where Carter Roberts lived between the wars.

At the back of this was where the farm pigs were kept, and there were stables for four horses. The area covered by Carter Roberts's house and the outhouses surrounding it occupies a large space, bigger in fact than that covered by the main farm and its buildings. This suggests that perhaps in earlier times, the Roberts's house was itself a separate smallholding.

The three cottages behind the outbuildings of Arne Farm. They were the homes of the Elmes, Holland and Gardner families.

Opposite on the other side of the road was Carter Roberts' garden. It stretched right up the hillside, and its banks were all full of primroses in early Spring.

Some distance behind this were three cottages, now made into one house. Here in the interwar years lived Mr. and Mrs. Elmes in the end cottage; George Holland, his wife and three children in the middle one; and Henry Gardner and his family in the last one.

Beyond them and sideways to the road stood the Dairy House, which the Royal Commission on Historical Monuments dated from the early seventeenth century. Today, the visitor can still see its early origin, for the lower part of its walls are made up of roughly hewn standstone blocks. From the end of the nineteenth century onwards, this was where all the milking for Arne Farm was carried out.

Downstairs there were four rooms and a hall, on one side of which was the dairyman's front room. On the other side of the hall was the kitchen with its stone floor, the range and the oven. A passage ran round the back of the kitchen to the milkhouse, which was the room next to the kitchen. Here, in the Smith's day, they made butter and cheese, for there was a large vat for separating the whey. They were very proud of their Dorset Blue Vinney. When the cheeses were ready they were stored in the cellar beneath the front room. At the end of the passage was an outer room with a large open fireplace, a pan boiler, and a bread oven. From this room stairs went up to a trapdoor in the floor of the cheese room above.

Upstairs, the main bedroom was over the front room, while over the kitchen were two rooms for the children. If they had any company come to

The village at Arne, seen from its ancient path to the harbour shore at Shipstal Point.

stay, then the children had to sleep in the cheese room. The Dairy House is a very old building. Was this at one time a separate farm?

The survey of 1825 mentions another farm of which there now is no trace; North Farm, tenanted by Hezekiah Talbot. It is not mentioned in the 1851 Census, though four years before, in March, Charles Groves had taken this farm on a yearly lease, paying £100 a year in rent. His name does not occur in 1851. His wife's does, so had her husband died in the meantime, or was he simply away for the census night? No name is given to her house. Ten years later, in 1861 George Boyt occurs as the tenant farmer here, occupying 200 acres and employing two men and three lads. Obviously, this was a substantial farm. Ten years later, in 1871, it has disappeared, perhaps incorporated into Arne Farm, with its farm buildings being used for the cattle. It presumably had become the Dairy House.

Behind it stood a large barn. Today this has been converted into an attractive holiday home. Across the road and standing back from it across the field called Park were a pair of semi-detached cottages. One was the home of Dorrie and Gladys Brown and their parents. In the adjoining house lived their uncle and his mother, the children's granny. After the Browns left in the early 1920s, Jimmy Hansford and his family moved in.

These two cottages were more recent than some in the village. They were of brick and had slate roofs. The front door of each house was at the side. It gave into a small hallway, which stuck out from the rectangular block. This led to the living room at the front and to the kitchen behind it. Going off from here was a small larder. Upstairs there were three bedrooms.These two houses were more spacious than many of the older properties. All the windows were latticed, like many others in the east Dorset area built during the latter part of the nineteenth century. A feature of each property was the shape of the fireplace; not flat at the top like most, but pointed like a church arch, according to Dorrie.

Arne Farm was the centre of the village, and from here tracks went off northwards to Russel Quay and the north part of the peninsula, and eastwards down to what were once fishermen's cottages at Shipstal, where there were oyster beds just off the shore. Today it is both a footpath down to the beach as well as a private road to the modern house that has been built there.

The track in the other direction to Russel Quay has as far back as people can remember been closed to the public In the eighteenth century, however, this was where clay from the pits in that area was loaded into ships for the distant potteries of Staffordshire. At times it would have been a very busy site. Today, because it is not open to the public, it is a very peaceful scene,

16

Charlie Battrick in a holiday pose, circa 1935, with Maisie Weeks from London, and his nephew Dennis Coombes, whose family lived in this cottage at Slepe.

with little except the waves and the gulls to disturb it, a great contrast to the modernity of Rockley and Hamworthy just across the water.

Almost on the water's edge are two huge pits now filled with water, where clay was once dug. Apparently, both are very deep. Phyl Marsh remembers an accident that happened here between the wars. "The men [from Arne Farm] were down there with a horse and cart. I don't know what they were doing, but there were lots of flies. The horse tried to get away, and must have put its head under the shafts. Before they could do anything, it started going backwards, and fell into the pit and was drowned."

The River Frome runs swift and treacherous here, making bathing dangerous. Not long before George Candy, who tenanted Arne Farm, died in the early years of the war, he had to go down to Russel Quay because someone was washed ashore there, and on an earlier occasion a member of Bonham-Carter's swimming party was drowned.

A couple of hundred yards south of the Quay were the remains of Churchill's Cottage. Built almost on the shore, it had by the end of the last century fallen down. Harry Clark says that his uncle could remember seeing the wall of the cottage still visible in the cliff, when he was a boy.

Back towards the village, another track used to go off in the opposite direction to Froxen and to Gold Point, where until this century there was at least one cottage.

Today few people are resident in the area, and those that do live here occupy less than ten houses, but a very different picture emerges from the 1851 Census. Then there were four distinct settlements in the parish. That grouped around the church, the farm and the school — Arne itself — was the largest. Forty-eight people lived here; that is, 40% of the area's population. Prominent among them was Joseph Boyt, who rented the 200-acre farm in the centre of the village. In the farmhouse, he lived with his wife, Eliza, and their eight children. These ranged from Henry, aged 18, to baby William, a year old. The family had one servant to help in the house, and four labourers on the farm. These were probably Robert White, Thomas Lockyer, Robert Masters, and William Main, who in 1851 described themselves as farm labourers and all lived within easy reach of the farm.

Just across the road was the village school where Jane Lockyer presided.

Almost as large as this settlement was that at Slepe. This seems today to be very surprising, as all Slepe consists of is one farm and one substantial but fairly new house. In 1851, it was truly a hamlet, as forty-three people lived here — 35% of the total population of the area.

Foremost among them was the bachelor George Stickland in his fifties, who leased the farm and lived with his two unmarried sisters. He employed two labourers to help him run the hundred acre farm. The rest of the inhabitants of this settlement lived nearby.

There was one cottage just off the Corfe Road where early in this century, the Patricks lived, and a cluster of five cottages about half a mile away and nearer to the harbour. Each of the five had two rooms downstairs, a living room and a scullery. Upstairs, there were two bedrooms but only one had a window. All five were very small, but large families were brought up in them. Florence Coombes remembered that her elder brothers had to sleep in the shed outside when the family got too big. Adjoining one of the cottages was a bakehouse which served all the families, and next to another was a fuelhouse.

Surrounding these dwellings was a very large garden, divided into areas for each family to cultivate, and sheltered from the weather by a stout hedge, in which grew plums, pears, russets, and damsons, and all kinds of fruit. Nearby were two other cottages.

All these have long since disappeared, leaving only their foundations, a few bricks, or an occasional bit of masonry to show where the walls once stood. In this cluster lived in 1851, 61-year-old James Fry and his family; Mary Selby, her daughter, and her illegitimate granddaughter; the widow Jane Crosson and her children; Charles Balson and his family; Thomas Coombes and his wife, who shared their home with George Chiseman and his wife; the Widow Furmage, and her son, who lived with another Balson, Thomas and his small family; William Pollard and his family; George Masters and his wife; and finally George Pollard, his wife and child.

Between Slepe and the main settlement at Arne, a little track ran down to another hamlet, at Coombe. There were four cottages here, all long since gone. In 1851, fifteen people eked out a living here [12.5% of the total]. Here could be found the Widow Stanfield, who was so poor that she had to be supported by the parish; William Chiseman and his brother, Charles, each with his wife and family; and finally, William Davis, his wife and three children.

The other substantial settlement was down at Shipstal, where there are still houses, but not the ones that another lot of Chisemans [James, John and Bethia and their families] would recognise, nor would the elderly George Gover and his wife, who also lived there in 1851.

Like most rural areas up and down the country at this time, most of those who lived here had been born in the parish, [53.7% of the total]. Of those who had not, the majority had come from the local area, from Wareham, Stoborough, Corfe Castle or Studland; all within a five mile radius. They made up 28.9% of the total. It was only a few [17.3%] who came from outside this area; from further afield in the Isle of Purbeck, or from along the Frome Valley. One came from Cranborne in the north-east corner of the county, and one had been born over the county border at Ringwood.

Again, as elsewhere, it was a comparatively young village; children forming a large percentage of the population; four out of every ten villagers were under the age of sixteen. Of these, twenty were under the age of two [16.2%]

For economic survival, every man had to work. Over the age of fifteen, there was only one man who did not. At 69, George Gover had retired, but no doubt he had spent all his earlier life working. Of course, it was the two farmers who employed most of the men. 38% of the total working male population were described in 1851 as farm labourers. A further 26% called themselves "labourers". These too may have worked on the farm, but it is more likely that they were employed in the claypits at Norden. The census does not mention clayworkers specifically. The rest — a large number, at 26% — were boatmen who supplied the area with the fish they had caught. Mainly they lived down at Shipstal or at Slepe.

If in 1851, practically every man had an occupation recorded against his name, the majority of women did not. It was specified in only nine out of the forty-one women over the age of fifteen. Hannah Furmage at Slepe took in washing. Mary White made buttons — a not very well rewarded job — helped by her daughter, aged thirteen. Sarah Randall described herself as a "householder", which sounds impressive and suggests she was substantially better off than most, but as she is recorded as living down at Coombe; and had a boatman son and his wife living with her; and the 1841 Census called her husband a waterman, perhaps she was not a woman of independent means, as the term first suggests. Likewise, Mary Chiseman at Shipstal called herself a "housekeeper", but as she only meant that she looked after her unmarried boatman brother, this was not a socially significant position as it would have been if she had been the housekeeper at, say, Kingston Lacy, or at Encombe. It was only the village schoolmistress, Jane Lockyer, could claim to have a socially better position, though perhaps not that much better off.

The other 80% of the women, what did they do? They were housewives, who washed, scrubbed, cleaned, had babies, look after them, brought them up, got the meals for the family, and if they had any spare time helped out in the garden. Worn out with constant children bearing, many died young. The Census of 1851 shows that there was a sharp drop in the numbers of women between forty and fifty from the previous age ranges. However, it also shows an increase in the numbers of women in their fifties, which suggests widowers were marrying a second time. Again, this is a pattern that could be repeated all over the country at that time.

Sources
Phyl Marsh; Reg Smith.
H. J. S. Clark for his memory of Canon Blackett.
The Census for 1851, as well as for 1841, 1861, 1871, 1881 and 1891.

The Candy family at Arne Farm, about 1910.
Grouped around Flora are Vera, Hubert, and George.

I
Farming

In the centre of the village in a very prominent position once stood Arne Farm. From 1894 until the early years of the Second World War it was tenanted by George Candy, and because he was here for so long, no one now remembers anything of the previous farmers.

George was not born here, but at Encombe where his father was steward for Lord Eldon, and where his uncle, Walter, was the Earl's agent.

With a lovely Dorset accent and a round reddish face, George was affectionately known as "Sugar" Candy. Lord Eldon sent him to spend some time training in Cirencester, perhaps at the Royal Agricultural College there, or may be on one of the farms that belonged to the earl's other estate at Stowell House near Northleach. Wherever it was, George learnt the art of farm management and veterinary techniques very thoroughly.

After some time, Lord Eldon made him the offer of managing a farm in the Cotswolds, but George had just become engaged to Flora Yearsley, who came from Southampton and whose uncle kept the Red Lion in Wareham. She was not keen at all to move away from her relations. So, instead, Lord Eldon suggested Arne, which was much more acceptable. The couple moved in shortly after their marriage in 1894.

A photograph taken some six years after their move shows the place as a substantial rectangular building, solid and old. How old we do not know, but its large irregularly shaped stone blocks which form the south and west walls suggest considerable age. At some point this ancient house had been extended eastward in brick. But when? Phyl Marsh, who was George's younger daughter, says that only the roof was altered just before her parents moved in, and yet the whole building must have virtually been rebuilt not long before that. The title-page drawing of the farm by Alfred Dawson, which appeared in 1882, shows the house as two buildings standing side by side. The western part, with its length along the roadside, had stone walls and was thatched, and the eastern part, behind the other and at right angles to it, had a stone, or possible a slate, roof. Such an arrangement may well have led to problems with rain water. Was this the reason that at some point the two houses were rearranged into one, with a new façade, new windows, and a new front door. If so, was the roof of thatch still left until just before the Candys arrived?

Rebuilding in Victorian times fits in with other developments, as farming seems to have prospered here as elsewhere during this period. This was mainly due at Arne to improvements in the soil made during the previous century. The

The farmhouse at Arne Farm, at the centre of the village, seen in 1902.

second edition of John Hutchins' *County History* claims that "since the beginning of this century" [the eighteenth] the land in the area had been "much improved with chalk imported hither." As a result, the ground which was once only suitable for growing rye "now affords good crops of wheat and oats."

It was not only this that had led to the improvements, for Barbara Kerr has shown how during the eighteenth century, the small lifeholdings that had existed here for centuries had been gradually bought up by outsiders. One such was Thomas Hyde from Poole, who had the wherewithall to invest in agricultural improvement. Later, his possessions had come into the hands of the Wareham lawyers, the Filliters, who in 1850 had sold out to John Scott, the second Earl of Eldon. He had also acquired the land of other smallholders, and, as he did so, he began to consolidate, so that by the 1870s only two farms remained, Arne and Slepe, in place of the innumerable small holdings that had characterised the village in previous centuries. As farming became more prosperous, so it would be natural for the house in the centre of the village to be rebuilt to reflect this prosperity.

In addition, the status of the tenant of this farm seems to have changed. In the 1851 Census, Joseph Boyt described himself as a plain "farmer", but twenty years later, in the census of that year, his successor, William Dominey, referred to himself as the "farm bailiff", as did Charles Smith who was here in 1891. Perhaps the alteration of the farmhouse buildings went with this seemingly more important position.

While they were at Arne, George and Flora's three children were born, Hubert, Vera and Phyl.

Their son went to Skewes' school in Wareham, cycling there daily, and when he left, Lloyds Bank in the town gave him a job. He was there when the Great War broke out in the summer of 1914, and like thousands of other young men he volunteered to fight for his country, and, like so many of them, he endured the horrors of trench warfare. For the rest of his life, he suffered from trench feet, and when he came back to England he had to soak them each night. During the fighting, a German bullet nearly killed him, but he reckoned that it was his silver cigarette box that saved him.

An efficient soldier, he was promoted to Lieutenant-Major with the 1st Dorset Regiment. Later on, he was severely gassed. After the war was over, he came back to his old job once more, but he became very ill and had to give up the bank. Later, he managed to get a job as a steward on board the ocean-going liner, *The Majestic*, and finished up as the Chief Steward.

Ten years after the Candys arrived at Arne, the whole of the front of the farmhouse and the western walls were covered in Virginia Creeper. It was a gorgeous sight in autumn as its leaves changed colour, but its eager growth was causing problems. It was getting under the eaves, so George had it cut down. A later picture of the house taken in 1923 shows the creeper confined

The back of the Arne Farm, painted by Brook Kitchin in the 1930s.
A new farm was built after the Second World War.

to only the side wall of the house, while the front has been rendered over, obscuring the stone and brick.

A small porch sheltered the front door, with two large Victorian sash windows on either side, and upstairs there were three similar windows, each with its own gable. The dining room was on one side of the central passageway, and the lounge on the other. Both faced south and were square shaped. Each had an open fire.

At the back of the dining room was the big kitchen. This may well have been incorporated part of the pre-Victorian house. It still had its hooks in the ceiling, where in previous centuries joints of meat and birds would have been hung, well out of the reach of vermin. All the cooking was done on a large kitchen range, just as it was in most country farms of any size at this time. Sometime later, Phyl recalls, her family replaced this with a smaller range, which had the open fire at one end. This alteration enabled the Candys to have a boiler, which gave them hot water in the bathroom, which was about this time moved upstairs. In this they were unique in the village, as no other house possessed a bathroom, let alone constant hot water to fill it.

Beyond the kitchen was the scullery, and in the corner of this was a large larder, crammed full. They always kept plenty of stock for anyone in the village who became ill, and egg custards were often made and sent to someone who was not well.

They did not have a cook, although when Phyl was at school a girl came in to do the rough work. One of these was Dorothy Coates, who came from Furzebrook. She was here in the 1920s. Evelyn Sheppard was another helper. She later went to work at the County Mental Hospital, at Herrison, near Dorchester. Looking after Phyl's mother, it was reckoned, had given her the confidence she need for her later job. Nellie Hansford, the carter's daughter, was another who came in and helped. When her mother became an invalid, Phyl took over the cooking and the kitchen.

For an important farmer like George Candy, there were always visitors, and therefore plenty of meals to prepare. Phyl remembers that their farm was an open house. A young nephew used to come and spend his summer holidays with them, and Flora's people came down regularly. Sometimes there could be as many as twenty-four people staying in the house!

Freddie Oakley, the corn-merchant, was a regular visitor. His warehouses stood prominently on the Quay at Poole, and were a hive of activity. Seymer Clark, Wareham's Town Clerk, was another who came in frequently. Others just popped in when ever they were passing. Canon Parish, who went from Wareham to Salisbury as an archdeacon, would call when he came back to the area. Doctors and policemen would also just drop in whenever they were in the village. No one was turned away.

Beaters and shooters at Arne —
George Holland, Henry Gardner, George Candy, Ray his nephew, and Cyril Ford, the keeper.

On Sunday afternoons, the postman who came to collect the mail would come and have a jug of homebrew, which was left for him outside. "Always a glass of beer, there," says Wink Sansom. "You were very unlucky if you didn't get a glass of beer when you went down there."

George made it on the premises, thirty-six gallons of it. The first brew produced a stout like drink, while the second was a light ale. He had a licence to do all this, but he was not allowed to sell any of it, so he just gave it away. The hops he used came all the way from Kent, but the balm only came from Blandford.

Every week in the winter, there were shooting parties. In the 1930s, they came in motorcars and used to arrive about 10 o'clock in the morning. In the earlier years, they would have come in their carriages, or by pony and trap.

The keeper on the estate went out with the visitors, and so did many of the farmworkers, who acted as beaters. One of these was Darky Courtney. Once, when they were out, he slipped and fell into a ditch and got all wet and dirty. For his trouble, George gave him a new pair of trousers. Darky said after this, that for another pair, he would do it again!

George's brother, Walter, used to come across from Encombe for these shoots. Owen Stevens was another regular. He came from Winterborne Zelston, and was George's brother-in-law. Mr. Jesty, who owned the watercress beds at Bere Regis and Warmwell, attended frequently, as did

Mr. Creech from the Blandford Brewery, who supplied George's balm for his homebrew, and very little stopped Freddie Oakley from coming over from Poole for the regular Wednesday gatherings.

The wildfowl that lived on the shores of the harbour were their objective. Quail, snipe, and widgeon were the favourites. At Christmas, it was the flocks of Norwegian ducks that came here that proved a great visual attraction, and the guns were laid aside.

After a good morning's exercise, when the men returned to the farm, dinner was ready; a big joint of beef and plenty of vegetables. Then, it was off out again to return just before it got dark. Scones, rock buns, and tea were waiting this time, with home-made jam. Phyl estimated that she made about a hundred pounds of it each year, from plums, strawberries, and other fruits they grew on the farm.

After tea, most of the visitors stayed on into the evening playing cards. It was not until half past nine or ten that they got into their motorcars again and drove off, taking with then whatever they had shot. Rabbits, and there were always plenty of them killed, they left behind for the farmworkers, whose families were no doubt very pleased.

Harry Clark's brother, Edward, was taught how to shoot by George. On his first lesson all he came back with was a rabbit. "You'll get a better one next time," said the farmer encouragingly, and this became a catch-phrase in the Clark household at Wareham for many years afterwards.

Fish was always plentiful on the Candys' table. Flora's sister had married a Bradshaw, who controlled the large fishwarehouse of Mowat in Southampton. Each week, he used to put on the one o'clock train a huge rush basket containing all kinds of fish, including crabs, lobsters, herrings, and kippers. It was enough to last a whole week. Someone from the farm had to meet the train at Wareham Station and collect the hamper. This weekly event continued even after Flora's husband died in the early years of the Second World War.

Opening off the hall of the farmhouse, and behind the lounge was the entrance to the cellar, supposed, according to legend to be an underground passage to the church. "We never found it," confessed Phyl, "but it was a lovely arched cellar." It was probably much older than the Victorian house above it, part of the ancient building that stood on the site. On its far side were five stone steps that led up to a wooden flap. This opened into the farmyard behind the house.

Beyond the cellar door was the Back'ouse, forming part of a lean-to at the back of the old house, where workers came after their long day's toil. Here they could enjoy a good game of shove-'a'p'ny, or darts, and wet their whistles with a jug of homebrew. The shove-'a'p'ny board used here was the long one that was only seen in the Isle of Purbeck, and not widely used outside that area. A good fire of peat warmed the room, and it was kept going all through the winter months. On a cold evening, it made the room very cosy and warm. In the fireplace above was a hook where a kettle used to hang. The Back'ouse provided somewhere for the men to go. There was nowhere else for them. The nearest pub was at Stoborough and that was a four mile walk away. This was on the spot, and no doubt their wives were less worried knowing they were up at Mr. Candy's, rather than at the pub. They would not roll home dead drunk, and they would not have spent most of their wages first.

In the corner of the room was a huge great copper, where on a Monday morning the laundry was washed. It was also where George brewed his homebrew, but every week the copper was used for boiling the clothes. The men used to light it up, and Lizzie Fiander, the shepherd's wife from Shipstal came up to do the washing. Wet or fine, she would walk up in her sandals. She stayed to have her lunch and then set off home again. After she died, Mrs. Orchard took over. She used to take the washing home with her to do, and Phyl would have to go down to Shipstal to collect the clean clothes. Later, when Phyl's schooldays were over, Nellie Hansford's mother used to come and do the laundry.

The Arne workforce —
Carter Roberts, poultryman Henry Gardner, and labourer Donald Barnes.

The area that the Candys had settled in had two farms, Arne in the centre of the hamlet, and Slepe to the east. Both were mixed farms just like most farms at this time. That is they grew cereals as well as rearing livestock, but whereas the farmers at Slepe carried out much of the work themselves, George Candy at Arne was, like this two predecessors, a gentleman farmer. His skills were in administration and organisation. It was his employees who put his plans into practice. On his land, the larger of the two farms, with 350 acres, herds were typical of many farms at that time, in that different breeds were all mixed together. Guernseys munched happily alongside blue and whites.

The Candys had not been at the farm long when Flora went down to the dairy to get some more milk as they had run out. It was quite dark. When she got back, George said to her:

"Did you see anyone?"

"Yes," his wife replied, "someone passed by. I said 'Good Evening,' but they didn't speak to me."

George turned round and said, "I don't like to tell you, but the bull has got loose!"

After that, Flora never ventured out alone at night!

She was not used to a country life. After all, she had been born in Andover in Hampshire and had spent a good deal of her life, before she was married, in Southampton, where she enjoyed the social life of a big town. She delighted in going to the theatre or to concerts. She loved especially the Savoy operas of W. S. Gilbert and Sir Arthur Sullivan. All this was missing at Wareham, which had no theatre and only the occasional concert by local amateurs, nothing professional as in Southampton. Yet in all the long years of her illness in later life, her daughter Phyl never remembers her mother being bitter about what she had had to give up in coming to live at Arne.

Milking was, of course, done by hand, and looked after by the dairyman. This was Maurice Chappell during the First World War period. Then came Job Smith in 1920. His father, Seth, was the tenant of Slepe Farm, and his other two sons were working for farmers around Corfe Castle. One Saturday when Job happened to slip into the Eldon Arms at Kingston [now the Scott Arms] on his was back from Corfe, the locals told him of the job going at Arne. He applied and was taken on as the dairyman. Later, in 1933, he took over his father's farm at Slepe, and his position at Arne went to a Mr. Best.

George Candy's cows were grazed in the fields around the village and along the south bank of the River Frome. These meadows which stretched nearly into Stoborough were locally known as Candy's Moor. Another grazing area was at Froxen, near the other end of the peninsula, north of the village. This is where English China Clays are now mining. The cattle's well-trodden path down across the heathland was, and still is, a feature of the landscape here.

Some areas of the grazing land were potentially very dangerous, with their thin marshy topsoil. Just before the war of 1939, one of the cows did get into difficulties in the quicksands and virtually disappeared. She was found two weeks later with just her head showing. She was still alive, and the workers managed to get her out again! Fortunately such incidents were very rare.

Slepe Farm probably was even more troubled by cows disappearing into the marshes. Its land, 170 acres, was considerably poorer than that of Arne Farm. Not only was much of it moorland, which in itself was not as good, but this was intersected by many dykes, and this was a constant worry. Many cows were lost.

Some of Arne farm milk was sold to the villagers who came to the Dairy House to get it. Eddie Anderson, then a newspaper boy from Wareham, recalls cycling down to Shipstal with milk from the dairy when he was delivering the Sunday papers in the 1930s. The Woods at Arne House had their milk from the dairy and expected it to be brought to the door, so one of the younger children — it was usually Jess or Nancy — who used to do this. If it was the lad, Mrs. Wood expected him to touch his cap to her when she opened the door. Often, she gave him something for his pains.

The Smiths turned some of the milk into butter and cheese. They were particularly proud of their Dorset Blue. The rest of the milk was taken out to Bank Gate where there was a wooden platform for the milk-churns. In the early years, these were collected by horse and cart. Later, Bill Cull took them away in his lorry. He came about 8 o'clock in the morning for them. Whichever way the churns went, they were delivered to the United Dairies' milk factory at Corfe. It was just behind the station, and was run by two brothers called Partridge. One was responsible for this depot and the other for the one at Sturminster Marshall. In later years, all the milk went there.

The Candys also kept other animals and birds. The large flock of sheep was the responsibility of Fred Fiander. Henry Gardner took charge of the numerous chicken and turkeys that were reared; about a thousand of the latter. He was proud of his success with them. Over the years they won a lot of prizes at Wareham. The birds were plucked in the Back'ouse in front of the fire, before being sent to market. The turkeys usually fetched about 2s 4d [11p] per pound.

At one time, the Candys also kept "gleanies", black and white chickens that could fly, but they did not last long. Every time the church bell rang, the birds would fly upon the roof and would keep squawking and making such a racket! They had to go!

George Candy with his chickens.

Turkeys at Arne Farm.

Ducks were much more acceptable, and therefore the Candys had a lot of them, as they did pigs. There was a whole row of sties for them behind Henry's cottage.

He had come to the farm when he left school and was a wonderful conscientious worker. When George Candy used to go out for the evening, on business, to Major Ryder's at Rempstone Hall, or over to Wareham for a dinner, or attending Yacht Club meetings, Henry would always keep popping into the farmhouse to ask, "Is the master back yet?"

Horses were essential to the running of any farm at this time. Ploughing, for instance, was still done by horses. The Candys had four and before they had a motorcar they had a chestnut horse called Trixie to pull their trap. Old Carter Roberts used to look after all the

Horse ploughman Fred Brown, father of Dorothy Churchill.

horses. He and his wife, Violet, lived in the substantial house behind the farm with their five children, Gertie, Kitty, Fred, Harry and Jim.

Fred Brown was another carter. He and his family lived in one of the cottages at Park.

The Tithe Map of 1845 shows small fields surrounding the houses, and one of the ways George Candy improved production and become more prosperous was to take out some of the hedges and make the fields larger. In this way more could be grown.

Perhaps the highlight of the agricultural year for the children was harvesting, particularly when the large threshing machine came noisily chugging over from Encombe to help. Dorrie Churchill [nee Brown] recalls the thrill of it. "At harvest time, we used to run home and take our dad's tea down to the fields and watch the threshing machine working."

Of course, Phyl Candy was not allowed to go and mix with the other children. Her mother would warn her of the danger that might happen if the leather driving belt slipped off its wheel, but nonetheless she used to sneak off down the fields. "I loved to see how it worked." In fact, all her father's workers were expected to turn out and give a hand.

Bill Brown, uncle of Dorothy Churchill, lived in the old house opposite brother Fred at Park.

Threshing at Arne had, naturally, to wait until the Earl of Eldon's own corn was finished at Encombe. "We went on a Monday morning and came back on the Friday," Wink Sansom now recalls. His father, Henry, had the task of driving the machine, which was appropriately named *The Earl of Eldon*, registration number FX 9237. With him and acting as his steersman, came Henry Gould.

One year, the young Wink Sansom came with his father, and he was even allowed to bring his friend, Dave Hunt. Another year, it was a different pal, Darky Courtney, who was allowed to come. "It was quite a treat for us," comments Wink. During the five days that they were in the village, they were lodged with some of the farmworkers. His father and Wink stayed with Jimmy Hansford and his wife, while his pal and Henry were with Carter Roberts.

It was hard work threshing, and certainly no holiday. They started each day early in the morning. It was a steam machine and his father had to get up a good head of steam before they started work. So as soon as it was light, "we were off." Wink's job was as "dust boy", that was keeping the straw away from the machine. It was pretty dirty work and he used to get very black.

Lunch was eaten in the fields, and there was another short afternoon break, about three o'clock, when George Candy sent down a large jug of his homebrew. Work continued on long into the evening. Only when the corn

Veterinary surgeon William Groves visiting from Corfe Castle in May 1912.

was stored away and his father had made up the fire in the engine for the night, that they could escape to their lodgings for a good wash and a sit-down meal. "We used to stay and have a yarn." For Wink, hard work it may have been, but it was fun he says, and he was keen to come again.

Afterwards, the straw was kept to be used for the cattle, and what was not much good was for the chickens. The corn itself was sold to the Oakley Brothers of Poole.

When it had finished at Arne, *The Earl of Eldon* and

The Earl of Eldon steam traction engine. This Garrett machine, 1910 works number 28758 and Dorset registration plate FX 9237, pictured at a rally at Hinton Admiral, in the New Forest.

Julia and Jess Smith at Slepe Farm. In the background is an old Bournemouth Corporation dust-cart, which they used for manure and mangels.

its team would chug off down the road to Slepe, where it was Jim Smith who often had the dubious pleasure of being the "dust boy".

As George Candy rented the land nearly down to Wareham, he was responsible for the river bank. Bert Courtney, Sam Holden, George Holland, and an old chap named Long, were often to be found along there, under the supervision of the gaffer, Ernest Prince. Flooding was a constant problem, and, to try to stop it, George Candy had a weir built at Redcliffe. The men dug out clots of earth and put in timber frames with wooden flaps all made out of elm wood. When the tide upstream, its force would keep the flaps closed, so the land behind would not be flooded. When the tide turned and flowed back out to the harbour, any water trapped behind the flaps could

Shipstal Point, seen from the harbour between the wars, when the Orchard family lived in the smaller cottage (opposite page). "Shepstal" is how it was captioned in their photograph album.

force them open and escape back into the river. Similar devices were installed at Criblake and at Black House.

The wood for all of them came from the Encombe estate yard and ordered from Mr. Loxton who was in charge. Just before the war in 1939, it arrived upon a lorry driven by Wink Sansom, now grown up, but still a regular visitor to the village.

Before this, in about 1927, Reg, one of Job Smith's sons, was taken on by George Candy, hoeing "mangels, swedes, and anything," but much of the time he was to be found with George Holland sawing down trees. Reg recalled that some of the trees they cut down were taken by the Encombe engine into Swanage and used repairing the pier.

At other times, George and Reg's work took them almost as far as Stoborough. Sometimes, Reg went and help construct the weirs on the riverbank. As he grew older, he learnt to plough using a three horse team. When George Candy acquired a tractor, it was Reg who learnt to drive it.

Peat was another commercial venture in the village, but not on the scale that farm produce was. At the end of the previous century when Frederick Fiander had married Elizabeth Chiseman, he described his occupation as a "peat cutter", but whether he did this to burn on the village hearths or for more commercial reasons is not known. It may well have been the latter, since it can be doubted if any of the local families would pay someone to cut peat when it was theirs for free.

Some of the peat between the wars, however, went up to Kew Gardens for the orchids there, although the Royal Horticultural Society's records do not contain sufficient detail to verify this. Some more went by train up to the market gardens of the Midlands. This was supplied by a Mr. Burgess, and his son, who had married into the Orchard family, who lived in the smaller of the two cottages at Shipstal Point. When they had cut the peat into blocks in the traditional way, they then loaded them onto wagons, which their horses pulled into Wareham Station. Later on, the two men moved their operations down to Goathorn, between Ower and Shell Bay.

Sources

Eva Biles; Dorrie Churchill; Gladys Clark; Dennis Coombes; Florence Coombes; Joan Jacobs; Phyl Marsh; Wink Sansom; Reg Smith; and Frank and Nancy Strowbridge.
Census Returns, 1851.
Arne Parish Registers.

Reg Smith on a ditcher on The Moors, dredging the water-courses.

II
Life In The Area Between The Wars

Arne was not entirely self sufficient. For many things it had to rely on outsiders, and in the days before the motorcar, workers often had to collect what they needed and carry it home manually. Farm-labourers, claypit men and fishermen had to walk four miles into Stoborough and Wareham and carry back whatever they could, as best they could. For example, when her family needed flour, it was Florence Battrick who was usually the one who was sent to Stoborough to get it. On one occasion, when she got back with the big sack and her mother opened it, to her horror, she discovered a nest of mice inside!

"I had to come right back from down there with the big bag of flour with mice in it for the baker to give me another bag," and then she had to get back to Slepe with it. In all she walked about nine miles.

For the Candys, it was much easier. They had a horse and trap, and much later on George brought a car. They could, if they wanted to, carry many more things, but shops in those days were prepared to deliver on receipt of an order. This system not only benefited the customer, but it helped the shop to extend its market and sell more.

Some retailers also had roundsmen who called round the village on certain days of the week. Bennetts of East Street in Wareham came on Mondays, Wednesdays and Fridays, with bread and groceries. Later on, their bread round was taken over by Bowles and Spencers, another Wareham bakery. On Tuesdays and Fridays, Dugdales in North Street called with meat. Less regularly came coal brought by Richards' lorries from Wareham Quay, and pots and pans from Welstead's shop at the far end of West Street. In later years, this service was taken over by "Oily Green", Percy Green, the mobile "paraffin man" from Ridge.

His van had sides that could be opened up to display a vast range of brushes, brooms, pots, pans, gardening tools and seeds as well as the paraffin, which was vital since all the houses in the village used oil-lamps when it grew dark.

Dennis Coombes can still recall his grandmother calling, "Trim the wick, father! It is smoking!"

Hurricane lamps were also common, so too were candles to go to bed with. The lamps, the candles and the oil were all supplied by "the paraffin man." Larger items such as tin baths, sinks, stoves and grates, he would order specifically for his customers from one of the many catalogues he carried.

*Percy Green was known as "Oily Green", because as well as delivering the Bovril and groceries
he also brought paraffin, from Ridge.*

Thursdays was his day in Arne. In addition, he often brought the Western
Gazette for his customers who had ordered it. His friendly chatter was for
many housewives a welcome break from their daily routine. It was also his
half-day, for even with visits to Stoborough and Ridge, he could usually get
finished by lunchtime.

Mondays, he went to the Lulworth area, and on Tuesdays he travelled to
Lytchett Matravers and the surrounding villages. It was, as his daughter
recalls, a "pig" of a road and took him all day and, sometimes, into the early
evening. Wednesdays saw him at the other Lytchett — Minster — and Upton,
while on Fridays he went over to Church Knowle and Furzebrook. Finally,
Saturday was for Wareham. "You wouldn't believe with the shops there
would be sufficient trade, but he did a good trade there."

Although he was exempt when war broke out in 1939, he had to join
up later. When he did so, his wife kept the business going for the rest of
the war.

Other visitors to Arne came less frequently, but a familiar sight in the
1920s was a Wareham man with a basket of fish. He was one of the Vyes.
Phyl Marsh remembers that her father always bought some fish from him
whether her family wanted it or not. Naturally, the man was offered a glass
of home-brewed when he came round. As he went round the village trying

Percy Green's replacement van.

to sell, he also bought up all the rabbit skins that the villagers had kept for him. This earnt them a little extra money.

Years later, when Phyl had moved into Wareham, he happened to be cutting her neighbour's hedge when he saw her struggling to dig up a lawn and turn it into a vegetable patch. He came across and insisted on doing this for her, saying that because her father had been so good to him when he was out of work in the depression after the First World War, he was only repaying a debt he felt he owed.

Fresh fish was also brought to the door by the Orchard children from Shipstal. Eight flat fish for a shilling [5p]; "lovely fish", as Nancy Strowbridge describes it. Some cottagers had no need to buy fish. They went out and caught their own.

Florence Battrick's dad was one of those who did so. Sometimes he used to take his daughter with him. In later years, he took her son, Dennis. His boat was a small pointed one, like a canoe. Dennis called it a "sharpshooter".

He then described how the old chap caught his fish. "We used to go out into the harbour by Slepe ... It's all grown over with weeds now ... and sit there till the tide goes down ... I used to have to sit in the boat and hold it steady, while the old man'd lay on the deck with his hands in the water till he could feel the fish over his hands. Then he'd flip them out. Behind him was a bath. I had to catch the fish and get them into the bath; flat fish. He used to get a bathful of fish. Then we used to wait till the tide came up and we used to row back with them. He used to pick them over. When he had enough, he'd throw the rest back."

Cockles were another delicacy that was going free. Fred Battrick and the other cottagers who lived near the harbour had a wire netting scoop that was always kept for cockles. With it, the sand would be raked for the shellfish. Winkles too were often caught.

Fred Battrick also had a twelve-bore shotgun, and he would go out now and then and shoot a couple of ducks. This was not unusual. Many other cottagers living near the shores of the harbour used to do the same.

Seagull eggs were another thing that Dennis Coombes also remembers his family going and collecting, thousands at a time. His mother used to tip about two dozen of them into the frying pan at the same time. They made a very tasty supper. At other times, Dennis raided lapwing [peewits, as they called them] nests on Candy's Moor, and brought back the eggs, "thousands of them". They also were fried or used to cook with. Other families did likewise. After all, these things were free, and there were no laws then stopping the practice.

"The daily round, the common task," for everyone began on Mondays with washing; the same for the Candys up at the Farm, who had a woman to come in and do it, as for the Browns at Park, the Battricks at Slepe, or the Smiths at Slepe Farm, who all had to do it themselves. Every indoor task took a back seat until the washing had been boiled in the copper, a deep sink set in brick and heated underneath with a fire.

Not every cottage had this sort of copper. Mrs. Brown boiled her washing in a large iron pot which she heated up on her kitchen range, and at Slepe Grannie Battrick's large copper pot was heated over a small fireplace next to the larger range. Above the fire a chain hung downwards, and on to this the huge copper pot had to be hauled when it was needed. When not in use, the area was covered by a wooden door, which was removed when in use.

It was the mother's job to light the copper fire if there was one, and fill it up with water, no easy task in itself in cottages where the water supply was not inside the house. Then the clothes were tumbled in and left to boil with Hudson's soap for hours. After a long time, they were hauled out. Grannie Battrick kept a special stick which she only used for this purpose. The clothes were then rinsed in cold water with a "blue" to enhance their whiteness, and afterwards they were put through the mangle. Some housewives, like Mrs. Brown, had to wring out all their washing by hand.

Next, they were hung out to dry. At Shipstal and Slepe, they were thrown over hedges and bushes. "Didn't have a clothesline; that was posh, wasn't it?" remarked Florence Coombes, and several other families did likewise. In the 1930s, by which time Florence had married, she was able to have a clothes line. Naturally, the Smiths and the Candys had clothes lines.

Blankets were difficult to wash, their size and weight made it awkward to use the copper. "Terrible" was the word Florence used to describe blanket-washing. Her mother used to take them down to the river and wash them there. That, she found was much easier.

If the day was wet, the damp articles were hung up before the fire.

Tuesday was inevitably ironing day, using heavy flat-irons, heated on the fire, tested on an elbow to make sure they were not too hot and wiped on a cloth to get rid of any black "smuts" that might get on the white clothes. Dorrie remembered her mother's methods. "Sometimes she held it up to her cheek to test. Sometimes, I've seen her wet her finger and touch the iron." For all of this, Arne was no different to any other place in the country — it was the same for the country mansion, like Shugborough in Staffordshire, or the overcrowded town house, as well as the rural cottage.

Because of all the fires needed for heating, cooking and washing, a lot of fuel was necessary. Coal could be bought, but it was far too expensive to be used when all around the area was a vast quantity of fuel for free. Wood was an obvious source. At Park, surrounded as it was with trees, Dorrie and Gladys Brown were expected to go to collect sticks. At Slepe, the Battricks got theirs from "The Plantation" close to Slepe Farm Pump House, getting through about half an acre a year. The young trees were then stacked upright against their cottage until Fred Coombes came to chop them into logs.

In addition, his son, Dennis, was frequently sent out with his brothers to collect "blackstocks". These were the blackened branches of furze bushes which had survived heath fires that were common in summer. His mother told him, "You must only have what you can break." He explained "If they didn't break off, she didn't want them. They were green. If they did break, they were dry, and we used to go and collect them."

Many cottagers also burnt peat. It was, like the furze bushes, all around. The Plantation was again a favourite place to go for this. When the heather died off, they went out with a turf spade and cut out blocks about two inches deep — all roots, all tangled up that it was like a "block of wood" [Dennis]. This "turf", as it was always called, was left to dry before it was used, but when it was put on the fire it gave out a great heat — "a lovely heat" [Reg], and in the mornings the ashes were thrown on the garden.

The reeds that grew in the lakes that bordered the harbour could also be cut down and dried to be used as fuel. Dennis remembers his grandfather scything the reeds in the upper part of Middlebere Lake near their cottage.

Other days of the week were devoted to the cleaning. Mrs. Brown at Park did her bedrooms on Wednesdays and her downstairs rooms on Thursdays, a pattern that was repeated in different combinations all over the country.

Again, the villagers of Arne were no different to those of anywhere else in how they cooked. In towns, the early part of the twentieth century saw the introduction of gas and then of electricity. In the countryside, it was still the black leaded iron kitchen range that was used. It provided all the heat for the small cottage. It made it "cosy and warm," according to Florence, when they were all shut in and the big fire was going, but its main function was to cook; large saucepans for stews and soups, and roasts in the oven at the side. All the food was cooked here.

Dennis recalls the puddings his mother made on the range, especially the treacle tarts, and suet puddings which were boiled in a cloth, and then tipped onto the plate, and sliced up. With a big tin of treacle or pot of honey on the table, "you could have what you liked. I'd always have treacle. Mother and father'd have honey." In winter, it was often boiled rice.

Then there was always a steaming kettle on top of the range. "When they wanted boiling water, you shifted him over. It soon boiled, since it was half hot all the time. Grannie's was hung up, but ours wasn't," explained Dennis, "Mother had a stick to slide him across, black as the House of Spades he was." His grandmother only needed to tip her hanging kettle slightly using a knitted kettle holder when she wanted to fill the teapot.

Some ranges had a boiler to heat water on one side of the fireplace. Florence recalled her mother cooking potatoes, cabbages and other vegetables in nets, which were all put in together, keeping them separate but economically using only one pot. At Slepe Farm, they had an oil stove as well as the range. Its seemed easier to use.

Bathnight was a favourite time for the children. For the Browns this was on Sundays, and the big tin bath that was always kept outside hanging up on a wall was brought in and filled with hot water. The children got in first, and Mrs. Brown would then be ready with a scrubbing brush so that she knew the children were quite clean when they finished. The water was topped up between each bather, and when everyone had had a good wash, their mother and father had to carry the bath and all its water carefully out and tip it in the garden. When they returned, they expected to see the children all in bed.

In an age before refrigeration was common, the people at Arne kept things fresh in their larder, which was usually in the coolest part of the house. In addition, there was usually a meat safe which was a large box with many air holes, small enough to keep out the large meat flies. The cooked joint could be put in it and it would keep for several days. The safe was usually hung up on the wall outside the cottage. Most families had one.

Many cottages had stone floors which needed regular scrubbing. Grannie Battrick used lumps of clay which her husband brought back from the claypits. These lumps were wetted and rubbed on the flagstones. It made them very white, "lily white". The Battricks could not afford carpets or mats to put on the top, nor could many other families. Some made their own rugs out of rags. Dorrie Churchill as a girl was shown how to do this using a needle to pull the rag strips through the canvas backing. Wool was rarely used as it was more expensive.

None of the cottages had water flushed toilets. At Slepe, each of the cottages had a lavatory down at the bottom of the garden, and it was just a piece of board with a hole in it across a bucket. The Browns' at Park was similar. Each evening Fred Battrick went down and dug a large hole in the garden to bury the contents of their bucket, so every morning it started off empty. Mr. Brown did the same at Park. At the Dairy House, the toilet was built behind a wall and down some steps, out of sight of the house. It too had a wooden seat, but it was across a pit, which was cleared out once a year.

Most villagers made their own bread. The Battricks made loaves about half a yard long in the little communal bakehouse at the corner of the cottages. This could be used by each family. At Park, Mrs. Brown had her bakehouse in the yard outside the backdoor, but she did not use it. Instead, she preferred the oven in her kitchen range. At the Dairy, Mrs. Smith did not make bread, although the house had an old oven, but she bought her bread from Bennetts of Wareham who called twice a week.

All the women made their own jam from the fruit which they grew or collected from the hedgerows around the village.

Many brewed their own beer. The Battricks made nine gallons of it at a time. In the 1930s, the men would hire a horse and cart from Reg Smith at the farm and go to Blandford to the brewery there for malt and hops. It would take them all day. Dennis remembers his dad's friends coming from all over for the beer-tasting on Sunday mornings when they crowded into the pantry to drink.

His family also made parsnip wine. "Grandfer'd swear by the parsnip wine. It was pretty powerful." Mead was another drink they made from the honey they collected. The Browns were another family who made wine, of all kinds, Dorrie relates, and her mother made beer only for Christmas and, so the children should not be left out, she made them a cordial.

Most mothers used to make their family's clothes, or at least as many as they could. Dorrie remembers that her mother used to get a pattern for their clothes, but since she had not been to school and learnt how to read, she had to look at it and work out for herself how it fitted together. Then she ran it up on her machine, an old Singer.

With so much work to be done, with no labour saving devices, and virtually everything having to be done by hand, children had to help. They had very little childhood or time to play. "Help?", exclaimed Dorrie, "Oh! My goodness, yes! We all had to help, even when I was at school, we all had our jobs to do ... We didn't get away with anything!"

"Never stopped!" commented Florence.

One of their tasks was to get the water for the household. Very few cottages had any form of water supply laid on. Arne House did. It was conveyed there through pipes from three large tanks which were supplied from a spring. The same pipes took water into Arne Farm, its dairy, Carter Roberts', the keeper's cottage, and to the schoolhouse.

Everyone else had to fetch their own. The Brown girls took buckets to a tank at the top of Park. This fifty yard journey they did after school each day. The Smiths when they were at the Dairy House went and collected theirs from a tap opposite the Gardner's cottage. One summer, this went dry and they had to bring in a water tank to keep them supplied. The cows, the milking and cheese-making must have taken a lot of water.

Over at Slepe, the Patricks got their water from a brook near their cottage.

Not far away from them, the Battricks, the Coombes, and the Orchards had a well of clear water in the garden which served all five cottages. It had a big bucket and chain to raise the water, and because

The Brown daughters, at Stoborough School. Gladys, left, was born in 1915, and Dorothy in 1917.

it was very dangerous, it was kept covered when not in use, and the children were forbidden to go anywhere near it. Therefore, it was the men's job to fill up the buckets before they went on to work each morning, carefully replacing the wooden cover and weighting it down with the large stone.

At Bank Gate, Reg Smith brought back a churn of water from Slepe Farm every night on his horse and cart for his family.

At Slepe Farm, this was one job that children did not need to do. The farm had its own supply. It was not mains water, but instead supplied by a pump in a galvanised shed, called grandly "The Pump House". This stood near The Plantation, just off the Corfe road. Every morning in the 'thirties, Reg Smith used to come down to start the engine. It was fed from a spring into a reservoir, from whence the force of gravity brought it down right inside the house. In dry weather, the water was often very brown in colour.

In addition, most cottagers collected rain water. At Slepe Cottages, the residents had two large half beer barrels each, though the Coombes could boast of a whole barrel. This water was very soft, and was very good for washing hair and for clothes. As a boy, Dennis was repeatedly warned to dip the bucket in very carefully when he was sent to collect some rainwater, and not to scoop it up quickly or he would bring up with it all the dirt and the sediment that fell to the bottom.

Collecting the milk was another job children did. Dorrie and Gladys Brown went across the road to get theirs from Arne Dairy. Dennis had to drop the milk bottles off at Slepe Farm on his way to school of a morning. They were, he recalls, just ordinary bottles, and Farmer Smith would have them filled up for him to collect on his way back. "Woe betide you if you forgot!". He had about four bottles, and was repeatedly warned by his mother not to touch a drop of the milk, as they used a lot in puddings and cakes. However, he and his brothers and sisters were terrified of the farmer, Job Smith. He was a great big man with a great black moustache, and if he was around they would not go and collect their milk!

On Saturdays, Dorrie and Gladys had to clean all the knives and peel the potatoes. On Sundays after their mother had prepared their dinner, they had to help her make cakes for tea. For Phyl Candy, cake making was also her task and a very frequent one with all the visitors to the farm.

Obviously on a farm, Nancy Smith's help was needed at an early age. She learnt to milk when she was eight, just as her brothers had done, and it had to be finished before she left for school. This meant she had to be up early — by seven o'clock at least — and dressed in her old clothes and boots. When she had completed the milking, she could have her breakfast, wash, change, and go out to catch the bus at 8.30. When she came back in the evenings, her mother insisted that she had a bite to eat before going milking again.

Arne families were perhaps much more fortunate than a good many others living in the overcrowded slums of an industrial town. Not only did they have plenty of fresh air and open spaces all around, but they had a variety of things to eat that cost very little money. It was a "lovely life", remarked Florence about her childhood at Slepe. Even though the menfolk did not earn very much — 9 shillings [45p.] a week was all her dad earned as a clayworker — they did not starve. They had a large garden to grow enough vegetables to feed his family well, and this applied to all the Arne cottagers. Mr. Brown at Park spent most of his evenings, when he could, out in the garden, so did Florence's dad. Later, when she was married, her husband often used to be down the garden late at night, with a hurricane lamp hung up in the apple trees so he could see.

As a girl, Florence had to pick out all the cinders from the garden and get it ready for her dad when he came home. She enjoyed this, as she liked being out of doors. Like most gardeners, he always set his potatoes on Good Friday, helped by his dog called Spot. If, when he came to the end of a row, he had run out of potatoes, he would send his dog to get another one and bring it to him. He had also trained Spot to run and get his tobacco from inside the house. With the right word of command, the dog would race off in obedience.

The old chap loved his garden, and it teemed with onions, runner beans, parsnips, and all manner of vegetables and fruit, gooseberries and rhubarb in plenty. His grandson, Dennis, recalls the rows and rows of blackcurrants he had. When they were ripe, his father used to write to Swanage and tell them the currants were ready. Then, everyone in his family had to help with the picking, so that basketloads were ready to be collected by a truck from Swanage.

The children were also forbidden to touch the ripening apples on the trees, "beautiful apples — russets". They too were destined for the market. Needless to say, Dennis and his brothers had a good feed when they thought everybody was out of the way.

Selling their produce at the market was a valuable source of extra in come for them. The Browns too had apples and plums, and Carter Roberts was well-known locally for his pears, which when they were ripe used to fall into his hedge. It was Dorrie and Gladys's job to go and pick them out.

Dennis' mother used to take him with her down the road to Corfe and pick pears from a large tree that still grows in the hedge along the side of the road.

Similarly, blackberries grew in abundance all around the village, and so did chestnuts. They cost nothing, and it all helped the economy.

Again, there were mushrooms all around, going free. In Little Mead for example, the large field to the east of the Patricks' cottage at Slepe, grew some lovely mushrooms, which the local cottagers were in the habit of gathering. They helped provide another source of food.

On Wednesdays, the girls had to help by darning the stockings and socks. Dorrie remembers that when they thought they had finished, they would shout " 'We've done them, mum!' She'd come along and look at it, and say 'There's a little hole there, and another there. When you've done that, you can go out to play.' "

None of the children got any pocket money, though it might be argued that they did not have any where to spend money. When Dorrie and Gladys's mother went to sell her eggs in Wareham market, she would call into Jay's shop on her way back and buy some little packets of sweet cigarettes and sherbet dabs. That was their Thursday treat.

Dennis had to carry big plates of cooked eels or cockles to sell outside the pubs in Corfe Castle on a Saturday or Sunday night. His grandfather often used to say, "We'll have eels for tea, mother!" Then, the old man would "put a nail through the eel's head on the bench and cut round its throat, slightly. He'd have a bit of white sand, very fine white sand on his hand, and he'd pull the skin off. Then, he'd cut off his head and the eel was still wriggling. Mother was waiting with the hot pan, and he'd throw 'im straight in the hot pan."

It was the same with the cockles. They were given a long soak in cold water, and then thrown still alive into the boiling water. Dennis recalls that they could hear the cockles screeching as they went under. After about ten minutes, they were taken out. "You had to take the shells off, and it always made me fingers itch". Any cockles and eels left over when the family had eaten were put on large plates and carried across the common to Corfe, where they were sold for twopence a plateful [less than 1p.].

Something else that used to bring in money was mole catching. Gladys' brother used to do this. He then had to skin them and put the pelts out to dry. He could get half a crown [12.5p] for sending them to London, and he could earn an extra penny [less than a halfpenny today] for each tail he sent.

One of the jobs that Dennis did not enjoy, perhaps because there was no money in it, was when he had to take a hammer and a big stone and smash up the cockleshells that were strewn over the garden path after they had cockles for tea. "They crunched every time you walked on them". When he had reduced them to a coarse grit, they were fed to the chickens.

Everyone kept chicken in those days. Some people kept hundreds. Mrs. Brown had a box which she had in her kitchen so she could keep newly hatched chicks warm. Not only were chickens a constant supply of eggs for many dishes, cakes, and custards, and they did not cost much to feed, but they also were a source of many a cheap meal. Dennis says he once saw Mrs. Battrick pick up a cockerel and chop its head off and let him run. He went round and round. "You've heard about it, but I've seen it! She used to wait about ten minutes and then out with its feathers, and that was for tea. They'd have the cockerel for tea."

Again, any surplus chickens and eggs could also be sent to market. Mrs. Brown pedalled all the way into Wareham on her bike with her eggs to sell them in the market.

It also helped the economy to keep a pig, and most cottagers did so, partly because pigs cost very little to feed. That was one great advantage. Another was that it provided endless cheap manure for the garden. When a pig had youngsters, they helped to keep the children amused and their mothers knew where they were. Dennis says he spent hours just looking at the little pigs. Most of them would end up in Wareham market, but in doing so would bring in a little more extra money for the family. All these things were important considerations.

Another advantage was that a pig gave so much when it was killed, providing a seemingly endless supply of food; pork, bacon, stews, roasts, sausages, and chidlins. The head and trotters helped to make nourishing soup. Nothing was allowed to go to waste. "I had to go for the blood for the black-puddings when the pig was dying. I had to keep stirring it. We used to make all the black-puddings and faggots," said Florence.

Her father, Fred Battrick, kept two pigs. The extra one paid for his rent — £4.50 a year to the Encombe Estate! Every year, they had to walk the pig over to Arne farm to serve the boar. Everyone did so. It was too expensive to buy a boar. Later, it was an important occasion when the pig was killed. It was not a pretty sight, and one that Mrs. Brown was horrified to find out that her children had been watching on one occasion, when they had slipped over to the Dairy House. Mrs. Brown did not consider that it was a spectacle suitable for children, and Dennis now agrees with her. Firstly, the animal had to be stuck, and then it was left to die. When it was supposed that the beast was dead, it was scalded all over with boiling water. Then it was hung up for about a day, before they began to cut it up. If the cottager did not perform the killing himself, it was a Mr. Thomas of Nundico in Wareham, who had to be sent for to carry out the task.

Another task that had to be done occasionally was to sweep the chimneys. It was the same method that was used for the Farm as for the cottages at Slepe. Reg Smith told the story about when he was working for Mr. Candy.

"Mr. George in the afternoon said, 'I want you, George [Holland] and you, Reg, to sweep the chimney, the kitchen chimney. You go up on Arne Hill and cut a holly bush suitable to drag up and down the chimney.'

George said, 'Right you are. We'll do that!'

We go up on Arne Hill and cut this bush with a nice stem that you could tie something on. We get it down and get the ladder up. That were my job to go up, a proper steeplejack. Anyway, we get to work and we went in the stables and got what they call 'plough-lines', what carters use for steering the horses when they are ploughing. We got two of them. Get to work; tied the plough-lines on. I had the bush up there; let the plough-line down for George and tucked the bush in. He was pulling it down and it pulled the soot down. Then he'd reverse and give a tug on my line, and I'd pull the bush back up. Then he'd pull him down again.

After a time or two, George said, 'I think we've cleaned it!'

Well, he cleaned up the soot all round the Rayburn. After breakfast, we cleared everything up, and went down sawing wood, waiting for orders after breakfast. Mr. George came up, red-faced. 'George', he said, 'I thought you knew better! Sweeping the chimney and not covering nothing up! There's all the stuff on the kitchen table and everything's covered in soot!'"

A similar method was used every November at Slepe cottages, though there it was slightly more difficult. Whereas at Arne Reg could get a ladder and climb on the slate roof, getting right up to the chimney, at Slepe the cottages had thatched roofs and they could not get right up to the chimney. Instead, the rope had to be thrown by someone on a ladder set against the wall aiming for the chimney. The line was weighted at one end to get it down the chimney. Great bunches of holly were tied on the rope, and these scraped the soot off. Then the holly was thrown out on the garden and burnt.

There was no midwife to help deliver babies until just before the First World War. The Liberal government set up the system as part of their series of social reforms. For centuries, it was someone in the locality who came to help, usually someone who had had practical experience of childbirth in the many babies she herself had borne. So, when Florence Coombes was born in January 1901, it was her grandmother, Lil Battrick, who assisted. She also was also brought in when Reg was due, to keep an eye on Mrs. Smith until the nurse could get to the farm. She kept going down from the bedroom and out to the gate to see if the nurse was coming across the common from Corfe.

However, later, when Mrs. Brown's girls were born, it was Nurse Tuck who came on her bike, with her long cloak, all the way from Wareham.

When Florence was married and about to give birth to her youngest son, she was informed by the midwife that she was not prepared to cycle all the way out to Slepe in February, so Florence had to go and stay with her friend, Mrs. Toop, who lived in Mill Lane, Wareham, until after Eddie was born. When he was fit enough, she took him back home to Slepe, and Dennis remembers they frequently used to push the baby in the pram into Wareham and back.

A new development in medical care that was being promoted nationally at the turn of the century was the provision of Isolation Hospitals. There is one such building on the road between Arne and Corfe. It was erected sometime between 1902 and 1904, by Wareham and Purbeck Rural District Council as a place where anyone with an infectious disease could be dealt with away from those suffering from other medical problems.

When it was first mooted, Wareham Borough Council were not at all sure whether such a hospital was needed for the town. They argued in 1902 that there was already an "infectious hospital" near the Union Workhouse at North Walls in the town, and had been been able to cope during the previous twenty years with only one patient! So was, they asked, the extra expense justified?

Two years later, the town changed its mind when a case of scarlet fever was diagnosed and the Council asked if they could use the hospital's services.

The Isolation Hospital, on the heath opposite the Halfway House,
after restoration by the National Trust.

The building that had, by 1904, been put up was a pre-fabricated one which was supplied by Humphreys of Knightsbridge in London. One of this type appears in their catalogue of 1900, according to James Grasby, of the National Trust.

The main strength of the buildings this firm supplied was that as a pre-fabricated unit it was quick to set up. In addition, they were flexible. They could be adapted to suit the site. The one here near Arne provided for twelve beds arranged in two wards.

But by the time this one was opened, the Local Government Board had become very critical of their construction. The Board had the supervision of medical care throughout the country, and therefore such hospitals came under its scrutiny. The criticisms it made highlighted the problems of keeping the buildings cool in summer; the noise of hail and rain thundering on the roof during storms; but, more seriously, their tendency to catch fire, partly, because the iron pipes from the stove passed unprotected through the matting of the roof. The suppliers did try to remedy some of these faults, and at Arne the chimneys are of brick, which was a significant improvement.

The Isolation Hospital here is typical of such hospitals provided by rural districts all over the country, but what is remarkable about this one is its survival. They were after all only meant to be temporary, with a life span of twenty to thirty years. Elsewhere they have been vanished. This one near Arne survives. The National Trust inherited in 1982 with Ralph Bankes's great estate and not only carefully restored it, but found a new use for it; as a holiday cottage!

How much difference did it make to the life of the villagers here? The answer is probably, it did not. There were few cases of smallpox or other dangerous diseases at Arne. These were more of an urban problem, rather than a rural one. It was usually for their infected patients that isolated sites like the one near Arne were chosen.

Sources
Dorrie Churchill; Gladys Clark; Dennis Coombes; Florence Coombes; H. J. S. Clark; Bob Dorey; George Holland; Phyl Marsh; Wink Sansom; Reg Smith; Nancy and Frank Strowbridge; and James Grasby, Assistant Historic Buildings Representative for Wessex, who supplied the information about the Isolation Hospital.

III

The Village School

Before Phyl's childhood, it had become the pattern for all children to attend school. Since the end of the nineteenth century, they had to. The law had gradually been tightened, and every child had to attend school until the age of twelve. By 1893, Dorset County Council had appointed an attendance officer to see that the law was being obeyed. He is first mentioned at Arne in the September of that year.

The village was fortunate in that it already had its own school. This was just opposite the church, and the building is still known as the School House. It had been, according to *Kelly's Directory* for 1907, erected in 1874 at the expense of Lord Eldon, but there had been a school in the village long before that. The Census of 1851 records Jane Lockyer as schoolmistress here, while ten years earlier the 1841 Census listed Jane Hall as being in charge.

A document among those at The Church of England Record Centre in London gives 1832 as the date when the school was first founded. At Dorchester, a church document of 1856 refers to it as a "parochial day school", and the Tithe Map of the 1840s shows the school as occupying the same site as the present school house. Was this pulled down and completely rebuilt, or just enlarged, by Lord Eldon? Just what did he do in 1874? He certainly owned the school, but at an early stage he seems to have linked it very closely with The National Society for Promoting the Education of the Poor in the Principles of the Established Church, to give the full title of the voluntary organisation set up in the early nineteenth century to found and run Anglican schools.

The names of some of the schoolteachers can be traced through the trade directories for the early period and after 1864 from the school log books.

1841   Jane HALL
1851   Jane LOCKYER
1873   Harriet SMITH; resigned because of ill-heath in 1877
1877   Elizabeth TURNER; resigned 1879
1879   Ellen or Eleanor CHAMMARD; resigned Dec 1885
1886   Laura WEBB; resigned July 1890
1890   Emilie DOWNES; resigned July 1898
1889   Miss DAVIS; resigned August 1900
1900   Mrs. THOMAS. A Welsh lady
?   Miss HARDING, died suddenly April 1902

1902   Mrs. THOMAS, again
1902   Miss F. A. MANSELL, resigned November 1903
1903   Harriette DUNN; resigned July 1906
1906   Florence SPEED; resigned September 1906
1906   Theresa CHILDS; resigned December 1910
1911   E. WALTERS, temporarily in charge
1911   Mrs. Georgina HOCKLEY; resigned April 1912
1912   Laura LILLINGTON; resigned four days after being in charge
1912   Mrs. Beatrice SLIPPER, who stayed until the school closed in 1922

This list suggests a large turn-over of staff. Was the village too isolated for them, too far from a town? Or, was it that a young schoolmistress suddenly found herself in sole charge of a school, with no one to turn to to discuss problems, and without much training for such responsibilities? Why did they not stay very long? We do not know, but, not counting the one who died suddenly, as many as five of the nineteen above stayed less than three years. Only two, bearing in mind the lack of detail before 1873, Emilie Downes and Mrs. Slipper, stayed any length of time; more than seven years, and Mrs. Slipper may have stayed longer if the school had not been closed. Obviously, because she taught those who went to school in the second decade of this century, it is Mrs. Slipper's name that crops up in people's memories today.

Most of the teachers were judged as competent by the inspectors sent each year by the government, and their reports, both for the school and its

Arne village in the 1920s. The School and Arne Farm, left to right in the middle distance, with the roof of the Church behind, in the centre.

The Schoolhouse (left) and School were under one roof, with a letterbox in situ (nearside corner).

pupils, were excellent, praising the work that had been taught. That for 1886 is typical. The inspector wrote "Good work, done by the late mistress [Ellen Chammard] has in every particular been carried on as efficiently by her successor" [Laura Webb]. Much the same could be found for most years right down until the school was closed in 1922. Ellen Chammard seems to have been the first to hold a certificate for teaching [in 1881], and after her time, every new appointment referred to herself in the log-book as being "certificated".

The *Kelly's Directory of 1907* mentioned above also says that the school could accommodate forty pupils. Lord Eldon was being over-optimistic about the size of his school, for numbers never reached that figure by a long way. The highest attendance was in November 1912, when it had an average for the week of 26 pupils, but numbers varied considerably. The lowest seems to have been in July 1903, when the average for that week reached only 10.3.

Whatever the figures, the children were taught in one room which was divided into two, half for the infants, and the other half for the rest of the pupils. There seems to have been an additional teacher as well as the schoolmistress. Their names are often missing, even though the fully qualified teachers are fairly well documented in the log books. Effie Northover was one of these additional helpers, so too, at different times, were Mrs. Slipper's sister and her own daughter [Alice]. Laura Briddle was an assistant there back in 1877. She had to take over the school when the mistress, Harriet Smith was very ill for some time.

In the infants department, the children learnt to write on slates, while the older ones used proper exercise books and pencils.

Like any village school up and down the country its progress was hampered by poor attendance. Many parents felt that it was more important for the children to help with agriculture than be learning in school, and Arne was no different in this. In August 1900, school numbers were low because the children were helping in the fields. In June 1893, it was to help with picking currants, and in July 1903, haymaking at Slepe kept the children of that area away.

Similarly, bad weather played havoc with the attendance. Stormy weather in November 1877 reduced numbers, so did the heavy rains of 1880; not surprisingly so since most children did not have the type of clothes needed to keep out heavy rain, and even if they had had them, it was three miles for the Slepe children to walk in, and they had to leave home by 8 o'clock if they were to arrive in time. From Slepe Cottages, a track ran up through Five Acres to Two Gates at the top of the hill, and then down again to join the road coming from Corfe. It was here they might meet the Smith children coming from their farm. Then, they followed the road to Bank Gate and by turning right they came into the Arne village. If they got soaked, they would have to stay in their wet clothes all day.

It is no wonder that if the weather was bad, they stayed at home. A heavy fall of snow in February 1879, another in January 1881, and another in March 1890 naturally reduced numbers, and the school had to be closed for a whole week in 1881 and again in 1890, but only for three days this time.

In addition, a very bad storm in November 1900 so filled the room with smoke and soot, that Miss Harding, who was then in charge was forced to send everyone home.

As today, illness could badly affect the size of the school. In September 1877, an outbreak of measles reduced numbers. The following March, it was whooping cough and other throat infections. Whooping cough returned throughout the January of 1880, and measles struck just over a year later, in March 1881. Ten years on, in February 1891, it was influenza that kept children away. This was following a week of heavy snow. After this, things seemed to get a lot better, for it is not until January 1921, that the log-books next mention the closing of the school on account of the weather or illness. At that time it was closed for two weeks on account of the influenza pandemic.

Occasionally, school had to be closed for other reasons and the children were given a day's holiday. In November 1892, Mr. Jackson wanted to use the building to collect the rents in. This set a precedent, and every year the children had a holiday when he came. The Royal Wedding of the future King George V and Princess Mary of Teck, in July 1893, closed the place, as did Queen Victoria's Diamond Jubilee in 1897. On 8th June 1900, the school was shut as it was the right-wing Primrose League's Fête at Wareham, and 12 November 1918 would be celebrated as Armistice Day.

In winter, afternoon school started at 1.30 and ended at twenty to four to enable those who lived outside the village to get home before it grew dark. This practice seems to have been started by Miss Ellen Chammard during her first term here, and it was continued by every mistress afterwards. A bad heath fire could also close the school early, as occurred in May 1915, when the children were dismissed at ten minutes past three "to enable them to get home in safety."

Some families' names keep on cropping up in the log books as infrequent attenders. The Bennett and the Battricks, both from Slepe, had bad records, but the distance they had to walk and the inadequacy of their clothes to keep out rain, snow and the cold, would naturally deter them. One of them, Alice, suffered from "bad eyes", and this often kept her away. In later years, her condition would have remedied with glasses, but at the time these would have been too expensive for the family to afford.

In addition, Dennis now admits that he and his friends played truant regularly. In autumn, they stayed away to go and search for chestnuts, which they enjoyed eating. When he returned home, his mother was under no illusions where he had been, and he usually got a clipped ear. But those chestnuts were, he felt, worth the pain!

A more unfortunate absence happened to George Holland when he scalded his foot. That kept him off school for several days in February 1914, and his sister was also forced to stay away to look after him. This was only two months before George came of age at fourteen and could leave school.

A much more serious accident occurred to Freda Orchard, who was terribly badly burned in November 1914. She lingered only a few days. Many children went to her funeral.

But there were children who attended very regularly. Laurence Orchard gained a medal and a prize for his record of unbroken attendance in 1906.

When they did come to school, discipline was severe. Florence Battrick still recalled as an old lady having her knuckles rapped by Miss Hawkins with a ruler. She said Florence was copying. But some children could be just as difficult then as now. One lad named Fred once tried to fight Mrs. Slipper! She locked the door and threatened to send for Canon Blackett, the respected Rector of Wareham, (whose commanding presence was enough to frighten most children!). She even dispatched her older daughter, Trixie, off to summon help, but eventually she managed to calm the lad down and the whole incident petered out.

On another occasion, Percy Northover ran home, when he was told off for being late. It was not the first time this had happened, neither the lateness nor the running away. His sister, Hester, also sulked when she was told off for a similar offence later that year. We do not know why these children could not get to school on time. Perhaps they had to come along way and felt it was not their fault. Clearly, life for children and for teachers could be difficult.

Less of a problem was Reg Smith's recollection that he used to sit in the corner next to Ernie Orchard and talk. Mrs. Slipper's usual way of dealing with this was to put Winnie Battrick between them. That often worked, but Reg and his friend used to get to other tricks. There used to be a mouse's hole in the corner where he sat, and when he and Ernie thought their teacher was not looking, they used to eat apples and stuff the cores down the hole!

With the various governments of the nineteenth century showing more and more of a concern for educating the working classes, the local gentry also took a keen interest in the work that went on and they were frequent visitors to the school. Lady Selina Bond often came in the 1870s, so did Mrs. Capel, the wife of the rector of Wareham. In September 1873, Reverend Hartley called to examine the pupils in arithmetic, and his wife often took scripture lessons in the 1870s. Reverend Pelham Stokes, a later rector of Wareham, was another frequent visitor, and on another occasion, a yachting party which had anchored at Shipstal decided to walk up to the school and see the children working at their lessons. Such visits must have had their drawbacks for the teachers!

Though at first it was reading, writing, arithmetic, and religious knowledge that formed the curriculum, gradually new ideas were creeping in. Class 1 began in February 1880 a study of the geography of Russia. Another new idea was tried out by Miss Harriett Dunn, who came to Arne at the end of 1903, when she took the school on a nature study in the nearby woods. In 1915, as the Great War started to be regarded as such, Mrs. Pinney who was one of the schoolmanagers suggested to Mrs. Slipper that she should take the children out to see the soldiers having a mock battle on the hills nearby.

However, it was not so much the lessons that our senior citizens now remember of their schooldays, but the annual treat, provided by the Earl of Eldon. "We were taken to Stoborough" in one of George Candy's wagons, all specially decorated up with ribbons and brasses and driven by Carter

Roberts. He drove them to a field off Nutcrack Lane. Here the children ran races, and also had swings. Reg Smith was privileged to go to the last Arne treat. He had left school the previous February, when he was thirteen. His father asked George Candy if the boy was entitled to go.

"Oh, yes!" George said. "He's entitled to go. He went to school for half a year. He's entitled to go and join in," so Reg went along.

His forte was jumping. He could out-jump any other boy. In fact, when he had gone to Kingston school, before the family came to the Dairy House, Walter Candy had refused to allow him to jump within his own age group. He was, Walter argued, too good. He had therefore put him with the older boys. Even so, Reg had come third. Now here at Arne in 1922 he had no competition, and went on jumping until he was the only one left. "I could either run under it (the bar) or jump over it," he now proudly comments. He reckons he had learnt his skill by jumping over gates and was following in his grandfather's footsteps. He too had had a reputation for jumping.

At some point, George Candy used to throw sweets, which fell into the grass and the fun began as the children rushed to find them; "scrambles" it was called. Then they lined up behind the Kingston Band and marched to the local school for tea. "It was only a slice of bread and butter and a little cake, but it seemed beautiful." Florence Battrick's mum used to help with this, as did other mothers who came along in Carter Roberts's wagon: "They were great times. They were fun." Dorrie Churchill still recalls the excitement of the events.

Empire Day was another big celebration in the calendar. It took place on 24th May which was the late Queen Victoria's birthday. George Holland remembered the school going on one of these days down to the shore for a paddle. For the return journey, the boys stuffed their long woolly socks into their boots, which they slung around their necks. As they came back, George stepped on an adder. How he got home he did not recall, but fortunately the baker was in the village on his rounds, so he rushed the lad up to Dr. Bell's surgery in North Street, Wareham. When they arrived, they were told the doctor had had to go over to Kimmeridge to a confinement, so George was carried across to the chemist's shop in South Street. There Leonard Ingrouille gave him something which knocked him right out. He did not come round until he was nearly home. Fortunately, the bite had no side effects.

Coming to school did help to raise the health of children nationally in the early twentieth century, through the provision of school dinners and medical inspections, though the former were never set up at Arne nor indeed at most village schools. During the Great War there are references to a school nurse paying regular visits to Arne School.

In April 1922, the Education Committee who now controlled the school decided to close it and move all the children up to Stoborough school. Jim Skears' small lorry now collected the children every day. There were three small benches in his van. It was "very bumpy," recalls Nancy Strowbridge, as the van bounded along the unmade-up chalky road into Stoborough, and back again. About seven or eight children had to walk from Slepe to wait for this "bus" at Bank Gate every day.

Sources
The Log Books for Arne School, D.C.R.O., MIC/R/891.
Dorrie Churchill; Gladys Clark; Florence and Dennis Coombes; Phyl Marsh; Tom Newberry; Nancy Strowbridge.
Information from the National Schools Society, *1995*.
Churchwardens' Accounts, D.C.R.O., PE/ARN;CW 1.
Trade Directories for 1841, 1851, and 1907.

IV
Off To Work

In the early part of this century, children left school at the age of thirteen or fourteen. For almost all of Arne's children and for most of the others all over the country, they left to get a job since their parents needed the extra few shillings that they earnt to help keep the rest of the family. The only exceptions to this in the village were the Candys. Their parents could afford to keep them on at school. For everyone else, work came at about the age of fourteen. George Holland, for example, found a job at Holme Priory, the other side of Wareham, for Mrs. Penn-Memeley. As it was five miles away from where he lived, he used to cycle there.

He started as a garden boy at 3s 6d [17^1/$_2$p] a week. "The first job I had was scrubbing flower pots. Icy cold water, it was, and a stiff brush." He worked from six in the morning to six at night. Later, George found another job, this time on Marsh's farm at Ridge, earning 5 shillings [25p] a week.

In 1914, Albert Gould left school. He was a year younger than George. He was not quite thirteen, but even so he found a job, filling a gap left by men who had joined up to serve their country. Perhaps that is why he was able to leave before his birthday.

By the time Reg Smith came to leave, it was the early 'twenties, and it was much more difficult to find a job, even though his father was dairyman at Arne Farm. Farming was no longer very prosperous. At first, his father found a job for him at the dairy, but when his brother, Jess, came to leave school, Reg had to go elsewhere, so Jess could have his job. He thought of trying the stone quarries to see if they had any work, but he was told that most of the jobs there had been taken over by men from Wales who had come to Dorset because they could not find work down the coalmines in Wales. Reg was told to go back to farming.

Sometime later, George Candy asked after him when he was

Julia "Kit" Smith and husband Reg hoeing mangels at Slepe Farm in the 1930s.

talking to his father. When he discovered that Reg was out of work, he offered him a job on his farm, so Reg started work for the Candys.

Other village lads found work in the claypits, just as their forefathers had done before them. Dennis Coombes, for example, followed his grandfather in this trade.

For the girls it was not farm work, but domestic service that was the traditional avenue. Lil Battrick sent her daughter, Florence, to Swanage as a servant, and when she left there, Lil packed her off to London to be a kitchenmaid in the South Western Hotel at Wimbledon. To get there, she had to travel by train to Waterloo, and change for Wimbledon. No one met her at the station: "I didn't know anyone there."

Her duties were to help in the kitchen for about three hours during lunchtime lifting big heavy saucepans. Before that she had to make all the beds. After she had done all this, "then we had an hour off, and then we had to lay tea for the barmaids, [there were seven of them], to come and have their tea. It was hard work, really hard work. Once a fortnight, we had Sunday afternoon off." For all this, her wage was only one shilling [5p] a week, when she started, but over the two or three years she was there, it did go up to ten shillings [50p] a week.

Things were different for Phyl Candy. She was the daughter of the village's leading farmer, and so she was able to stay on at school to complete her education. Like all the other children, she went to the local school at an early age — three, but when that closed, her mother wanted to send her to Skewes' in Wareham, run by Mrs. Candy's cousins. Her mother hoped the council would allow her daughter to ride into Stoborough with the other children going to the school there, but the council refused. Therefore, Phyl was sent to stay with her older brother, Bert, and his wife in Poole, where she could attend Parkstone High School, the girls' grammar school for the area. She stayed there until she was ten.

Then she came back to the Isle of Purbeck to board at Sunningdown School in the centre of Swanage. Because of its site, which was right on the water's edge, it had its own private beach. It also had several tennis courts, where Phyl learned to play. The school was run by its Head Mistress, Miss Ruth Dawson, with her sister, Miss Ballard Dawson, a keen Methodist preacher. In addition, there were three other teachers.

Among the friends Phyl made there were "Brownie" Berridge, whose family had rubber plantations in the Far East, Elizabeth Nutt, whose father was a doctor in Norwich, "Peter" Fields from Launceston in Cornwall, Thelma Proust, and Margaret Gibson from the West Country. Clearly, the school drew its pupils from a very wide area.

In addition to the academic studies, the girls were encouraged to join the choir, and also to learn folk dancing. Every year there was a big competition at the Bournemouth Winter Gardens in the latter.

Since most of the girls, it was supposed, would eventually be in charge of an important household, practical skills in laying the table and in making beds were given.

Just after Phyl left, the school moved inland to Langton Matravers. For some time before this, the Hotel Grosvenor, which was next to the school, had had its eye on its neighbour, which commanded a prominent site adjoining the hotel, so the Dawsons sold out and The Grosvenor took over and expanded. The new location at Langton had some obvious advantages for the school in that it had plenty of nearby fields for the girls to play on.

Again unlike her contemporaries in the village, Phyl was not expected to find a job. It was still not acceptable for prosperous farmers' daughters to want a career. She had plenty of time, and she used to go visiting relatives and friends a lot. She often went up to Southampton to stay with her mother's brother-in-law, Uncle Will. He had a huge fish warehouse Below Bar and a shop up the Avenue. He was the one who used to send the weekly hamper of fish to her parents. In addition, he supplied all the important liners of the period with fresh fish, and the years between the wars were the heyday of the great liners. In the warehouse, Phyl used to go and inspect the underground chambers where they had shelf after shelf of crabs, lobsters and all kinds of other fish, which were kept alive in the warehouse and subsequently could be taken on board still alive. Liners wanted to serve fish as fresh as possible.

Phyl also went across to Hewish Manor, near Winterborne Zelston, when Owen Stevens was there. He had married her father's sister, and a visit there was quite an experience, since they had a pool in the cellars. Later, Owen sold Hewish and moved into Wimborne. He was quite an important man. He invented the hedge-cutter and the hay-sweeper.

Another place Phyl went to stay was at Midhurst. Here lived an "Aunty and Uncle", the Caves, who had been at Rempstone Farm before they moved to Surrey. Nearby, there was a field where Phyl would often see the Duchess of Bedford bringing her plane in to land. While Phyl stayed with the Caves they would often take her to Goodwood Races and to Petworth House.

That Phyl did find employment was due to unforeseen circumstances. Her brother had married a Myers, whose brother was a dental surgeon in Poole. He also had a practice in Wareham above Symonds' printing and stationery shop in West Street. Harry Clark recalls him always seeming to have his hat on! One Sunday morning, he came into the Candys' house "in an awful state ... because he had not got anyone to take over the nurse's job." She was leaving to get married.

As he spoke, Phyl casually said, "Oh! I'd like that!"

Mr. Myers turned to her and asked, "Do you mean that?"

"Mother said, 'Why don't you go? Don't stop for me.'

The Candys had a girl working in the house and a woman who came up in the evenings to do anything, so her mother felt she could manage.

The following Sunday, Mr. Myers came over and picked her up in his car. She stayed with him for two years, until her mother grew worse and she had to return home to look after her. During those two years, "I had a marvellous time!"

In addition, Mr. Myers used to do dental work at Cornelia Hospital, now Poole General, and Phyl used to go there with him. Off duty, a wide social life opened for her. Mr. Myers used to take her and Nurse Gwen Lambert, who later became matron at the hospital, to dances at the Royal Bath Hotel in Bournemouth, and he used to take a couple of doctors with them as partners. Phyl now confesses that thanks to her friends, "I had a wonderful time!"

Sources
Florence Coombes; Dennis Coombes; George Holland; Phyl Marsh.
The Log Books of Arne School, D.C.R.O., MIC/R/891.

V

Leisure

The beach at Shipstal Point, in a calendar picture of the 1930s,
before spartina cord-grass encroached along the shoreline.

In spite of having so much to do, children did seem content. They had to make the most of what little spare time they had. "We never said we were bored," commented Dorrie Churchill. "We made our own amusement", added her sister, Gladys, and this would have been supported by almost all the children in Arne. Florence Coombes, as a girl, played a bit of skipping and hopscotch, and her son, Dennis, was happy to kick a ball around, and, although there were not enough boys near him to have a serious game, he and his friends nevertheless enjoyed playing football. Usually, they did so on the Bank, a large field close by the cottages at Slepe. His mother was happy with him here, and used to warn her son not to wander away from there. At other times, she was content with Dennis going with his brother fishing at Sheerlake, the bridge where a little stream runs under the road to Slepe Farm.

At the farm, Nancy Smith also found time to play "houses" with a few old tin cans and kettles up in the woods, while Gladys Brown was usually up trees, and, as often as not, falling out of them, though she cannot remember being really hurt. Once she did climb up in her Sunday best after they had come out of church. Her mother, not unnaturally, was very cross! At night,

Dorrie and Gladys would often go out into the woods behind their cottage and run among the trees, shouting "Midnight Donkey won't be out tonight!"

Occasionally, sheer high spirits led to mischief, as when Dennis and his friend, one of the Orchards, found a piece of rope which belonged to Reg Smith, who was now back at the farm, and they hid it. Sometime later, Reg came up and enquired "Have you two buggers seen my rope?"

They replied looking all so innocent "No, we haven't seen no rope!"

"He knew we had it," Dennis later recalled, "and he found it. He gave us a good hiding, but we begged him, 'Please, don't tell father!'"

Although the beach was on their doorstep, it held no particular attraction for Arne children. They did not spend much of their leisure time down on the shore. Nancy Smith does not remember going down there much at all. Even if they did go, they were not allowed to bathe. They could go paddling if an adult was with them. Naturally, one day, Dorrie Brown did venture in, and on their return home when her sister told their mother, she was furious, and the culprit was sent off to bed. Perhaps, boys were allowed more freedom. No one told Dennis Coombes off for plunging into Middlebere Lake during a hot summer, which he often did, but the water was, he recalls, very muddy.

Two events have stuck in Dorrie's memory. One was when a car broke down in the village, and as a car was still, in the 'twenties, a very unusual sight, especially one broken down, Dorrie and her sister ran down to see what had happened. They hid among the bushes and watched with delight as the vehicle was towed away by horses: "Don't know whose car it was, but we really enjoyed the sight."

The other occasion was when a small plane ran out of fuel and had to make an emergency landing on the heath between the village and Russel Quay. "I can't remember when it happened, but my sister said my Uncle George sat me in the seat of the plane."

In winter months, the Browns often used to sit at home and watch the fire, and during these months the Coombes played cards.

Birthdays were not specially marked, so that when Dorrie had a present for her fifth birthday, it was something that remained in her memory. "I can remember now putting my hand up to the table and taking this new cup and saucer." She does not recall having any cards, but if she had they would have been hand-made.

Christmas was special for the Browns. Their mother always had a tree at the bottom of the stairs: "One Christmas, we all had 'flu, so all we could do was to look down from the landing at this tree." Normally, the girls would have made the decorations for it and hung them on the branches. They also made paper chains to hang around their living room, as did Nancy Smith at her parent's farm. No doubt all the other families did the same. Stockings were hung up for Father Christmas to fill, and the children's excitement mounted the next morning as their little fingers felt the outside of the woolly sock trying to discover what was inside. Not that there would have been anything costly; nuts, sweets, and other little things, all wrapped up in little paper parcels, and, of course, an orange, usually right down at the toe of the stocking.

For the festival, there was always plenty to eat. Their mothers had seen to that, for they had been busy making pies, puddings and cakes for many days before. It was a time when friends and family visited each other. The Browns' Aunty and Uncle who only lived next door came round.

At Arne Farm, there were more visitors. Flora Candy's sisters, Mary, Jessie, and Julie, used to come over. As Phyl grew older and her circle of friends widened, she would often go over to the Marshes at South Bestwall Farm on Christmas Eve and New Year's Eve, and join a big party there. At this time in the 'thirties, she recalls, it seemed the fashion to give chocolates. One year she had thirteen pounds!

"You're not having all those chocolates", declared her mother, who allowed her to keep only a few boxes. The rest were given away as Christmas boxes to people in the village.

But horizons were widening for everyone in that period between the wars. The Battricks had both an old gramophone and a radio set. The latter was worked by an accumulator, which generated the electricity for the set. However, as they needed recharging once a week, most households had two accumulators, one working the radio and the other being recharged. It was Dennis's job to take the run-down battery into Wareham on his bike to the Modern Radio shop in West Street, and collect it again when it was sufficiently recharged. Mr. and Mrs. Burt who ran the shop charged 6d [2 ¹/₂p] for this service.

The assistant, a man named Devon, would take it from him. He knew which accumulator belonged to whom. Dennis recalls "One day, I was cycling back, and the thing fell off and smashed. I didn't know how to face grandfer. He never had a spare, and a new one was out of the question."

Somehow he made the old chap understand.

His own parents didn't listen to the radio very much, though they all liked hearing "The News". When it was over, his grandmother would say, "Shut that off! We can't afford no more!" or, "Put a cork in that man's mouth!"

Apart from "The News", they occasionally liked a music hall if someone they liked was on the bill. But the presence of the radio was opening up a much wider vision and gaining for them more of a knowledge of the world as a whole.

Everyone walked, and many would think nothing of walking into Wareham or Corfe Castle. Dennis's grandparents regularly went into market on foot, and the couple of miles from Slepe into Arne was nothing. His grandfather went into Arne every day to visit the Orchards down at Shipstal whom they knew very well, or to have a drink in the backh'us of Candy's farm; and walk back again. This was so regular that they regarded it as nothing. Once when his father's sister and her husband came down to stay with them for a week's holiday, they took their visitors to Corfe and back. The Londoners vowed they would never come to Slepe again. They had never walked so far in one day before! They were not used to it, whereas everyone in Arne, and in the countryside generally at this time, was.

Dennis and his family often went to Swanage. It was very cheap on the railway. His mother would give him 2d [¹/₂p] for the day return ticket! He had to walk to Corfe, of course, to catch the train, and walk back again in the evening, but that was regarded as perfectly acceptable. "A marvellous day!", he calls it!

Another factor in lessening distances in the 1930s was the popularity of the push bike, although this had been around for more than half a century. By this time, most boys had bikes. They enabled young men to get away from the normal confines of the village. Many men from the area used them to get to work every day in the cordite factory at Holton Heath. By riding their bikes, Reg Smith and his friends could be regulars in Wareham at the New Inn on the Quay, or at the Black Bear. They did not have a lot to drink but they did learn to smoke. A packet of Gold Flake, a popular cigarette brand of the period, could be made to last a week.

Even before this, many of them had had an old bike — usually it had only the very basis essentials, and did not have any brakes. The boys would ride up and down a sloping field, plunging into the bushes at the bottom.

A push-bike enabled Dennis's grandfather to get into Wareham market much easier, do his shopping, have a couple of pints at the Antelope, and buy an ounce of Black Boy Tobacco before going back home.

For Phyl Candy, a bike enabled her to ride all over the local area. It meant she could cycle, for example, to Wareham Station and catch a train to Poole, where she could go and see a film. The people who owned the Regent Cinema there [Geoff Bravery and his wife] were friends of her father's, and she was welcomed to see what was showing at any time. Afterwards, she caught the train back to Wareham, found her bike, and then cycled home.

She also used her bike to visit her friends, like the Knights of Middlebere Farm, for example. To get there, she had to cross a stream on a couple of planks. On one occasion, the tide was exceptionally high and when she

The Knights from Middlebere Farm, pictured on a visit to Arne Farm.
Mrs. Frances Knight (second from left) with her sister-in-law, her brother, son Ernest,
and daughters Leah and Joyce.

came to go back, she found that it was impossible. Her friends' son, Ernest, told her not to worry as he would take her back on his motorbike, but the tide was too high even for his machine, so she had to spend the night at Middlebere. Her anxious father was extremely cross when she did reach home. He was waiting up for her. When her friends heard about the incident, she was teased for a long time afterwards, with their comment, "...Came to a river and couldn't get across!"

It was his bike that enabled Jim Strowbridge to court Nancy Smith. Whereas the previous generation of girls tended to marry men within the Arne — Corfe area, Jim met Nancy at Wareham Fair. She remembers the swinging boats going out right over the river. Jim lived towards Lulworth and worked in the Frome valley on a potato farm at Woodsford. After he had finished of an evening, he would cycle home to Lulworth, wash and change, then go and meet Nancy. He often took her to a Sixpenny Hop — at Tyneham, Creech Grange, or in the Drill Hall at Wareham. It might be three o'clock in the morning before he got his girlfriend back to Slepe. Then he had to cycle back to Lulworth, where he had to be up at four o'clock to be at work for six a.m. It was the bike that enabled him to lead such a fast life, and the fact that Sixpenny Hops did not happen every evening.

These Hops were very popular in the period between the wars, drawing crowds of teenagers. Those at Kingston are well remembered, with Bill Damer at the piano, John Riddle on the banjo, Ken Orchard on drums, Gerald White on the trumpet, and Una Smith and Miss Cleall on the violins. Sometimes there was even a chap from Stoborough on the bass.If these Hops drew the younger farm workers, there were also plenty of more formal dances for the affluent. Phyl Candy was often taken out to such evenings.

She also enjoyed playing tennis, which few of the labourers could could indulge in. She had learnt to play at school, and there were courts at Bestwall House in Wareham, at the Durrant Lewis's, at the Millers' and at Arne House that she could play on.

The increasing passion for mobility affected her parents, and her father bought a motorcar — an FX [the original Dorset registration letters]. His brother-in-law, Owen Stevens, taught him how to drive. One day, not long after this, Reg Smith "was driving the cows in from a field up Salterns Wood, all across the common and along the main road into Arne," when George came up behind in his new car.

"I don't think he was too familiar with the brakes and he hit the cow's back leg — didn't do much damage, but later he came hurrrying down to the dairy, very concerned and asked Job Smith, 'I hit a cow's leg. Have I done any damage?'"

Reg had to say which cow it was. He looked at the cow, but he hadn't done any damage, "just slided into it."

Changing the car's tyres was another job that Reg was asked to do.

However, in the 1930s, it was owning a motorbike that was the dream of most young men. Among the older generation, Dennis's father was unusual in that he possessed such a bike. This may have been because he was Londoner and before his marriage would have been aware of the new machines long before they reached Arne. When his bike got old and started playing up, Reg Smith bought it, and enterprisingly took off the back tyre, put a belt on, and used it for driving his chaff cutter.

Nancy Smith, the daughter of Job Smith at Slepe Farm, courted Jim Strowbridge.

Mauson Marsh on his motorcycle on heathland near High Tor, Samuel Cottee's house at Holme Bridge, on a Sunday in June, 1934.

Reg also had his own bike. Later, when he had done it up, he had his eyes on a better machine, so he sold the first one to Tom Battrick for £5, but when Tom came to get it, he only had £4. Since Reg had spent a lot of time on it, he said, "Well, that isn't enough!"

Mauson Marsh and brother Fred, standing, with Bill and Stanley Pond seated on the bike, at High Tor.

George Candy's first car, Dorset registration number FX 3721, with the owner (right), sister Jessie Stevens, wife Flora, and brother Walter.

"Well," said Tom, "I'll go home and get some more."

When he came back, he had in his hands his father's double barrelled gun that he used to go duck shooting with, and offered Reg that to make up the balance. Reg was very pleased with such a bargain, and so, in his own words, "because I got the gun, I let him have the bike. Before the day was out, his father came back with the money and wanted his gun back."

Motorbikes meant that Reg and other young men could go further afield — as far as Poole or to Swanage. It was at Swanage during one of these excursions that on the seafront he met his future wife, Julie [or Kit as she was always known].

For the older generation, who did not have bikes, it was a question of walking, especially if they did not want to get their drink up at George Candy's back'ouse. Then they would have to walk the three or four miles to Stoborough or Wareham.

Certain of the families in the village did this as a matter of course, and often if their neighbours met any of them as they staggered back, it would have been obvious as to where they had been. On one occasion, a passer-by found several members of one family all laid out in a ditch, dead-drunk, but otherwise none the worse!

Another regular chance for a drink occurred during the annual visit of the territorials to camp at Furzebrook. Many of the Slepe families walked across

Reg Smith on Bournemouth-registered RU 2809, at the Dairy House beside Arne Farm, in the 1920s.

the heath to sample the delights of their beer tent. It was an occasion that could not be missed!

Weddings were other welcomed events, and an excuse for a celebration. When Florence's brother, Charlie, married the daughter of the farmer at Worgret, the Coombes hired Reg Smith's horse and cart, and all the Slepe families piled on and went off to the wedding. Afterwards, everybody returned to Worgret for the reception. Dennis's eyes opened wide in amazement at the huge slices of roast beef that the farmer and his wife provided for their guests. It was certainly a day to remember!

Sources
Dorrie Churchill; Gladys Clark; Dennis Coombes; Florence Coombes; George Holland; Phyl Marsh; Wink Sansom; Reg Smith; Nancy and Frank Strowbridge.

VI
Church Activities

The bell that tolled out every Sunday calling the faithful to church had done so for centuries, although the present bell tower only dates from the seventeenth century. Experts tell us that the simple little building of chancel and nave had probably been built around 1200. Its windows are the typical lancets of that period, and structurally little has changed much over the intervening centuries, though one window in the south wall has been altered, probably in the fourteenth century, by making the top of it square. Another window was inserted when the bell tower was made three centuries later. A porch has also been added possibly in the thirteenth century. Other than this, there has been little structural alteration, mainly because Arne never grew that prosperous and, or, its population did not expand significantly.

Visually, however, the inside of the building has drastically changed. A medieval person would not recognise it, just as he would not recognise most other churches. The sixteenth century Reformation had devastating effects on the interiors of all churches throughout the kingdom. Before this time, the inside would have been alive with colour. Vestiges of the medieval wall paintings have been uncovered at Arne on the west wall, and over the

St. Nicholas's Church, in an Edwardian postcard, sent in 1909.

doorway there is a stencilled pattern in red paint, possibly showing pomegranates, which is thought to be early sixteenth century work. These two fragments hardly give us any real impression of the bright interior of that period. In addition, the colour of the priest's vestments and the altar frontals and the smell of the incense would have added to this brightness. Arne being a small parish would not have had the richness of choirs chanting the services.The one priest would have had to conduct the whole service himself.

All this was swept away at the Reformation, the colour, the latin, and the chanting, when Henry VIII broke with the pope in the 1530s, though for most of King Henry's reign the interior of the church would not have been drastically affected. The most noticeable change throughout the country was probably the abolition of the monasteries, and since Arne was owned by the Abbey of Shaftesbury, this should have meant a serious change. In practice, it may have been less drastic. In the immediate period, the villagers paid their rents to the King's officials. Later, when he sold the land to laymen, it would have been to them that the tenants at Arne now paid their rents. Perhaps, the change of owner did not mean very much. The tenants still had to pay their rents.

It was only under Henry's son, Edward VI, that the old services were altered. They were now to be in English and not in Latin. Interiors were to be whitewashed over, and the sermon to be a more important part of the service. We do not know what the villagers thought, and whatever it was it was not important to the king. It is also possible that Arne escaped most of these changes, as it was, and still is, off the beaten track. Today, it still has its medieval stone altar, whereas at many other places these were taken out and smashed by the reformers, and plain wooden tables set up in its place.

At some point, Arne's stone altar was removed and hidden below the floor. It was later found there, but it was not in pieces, so whoever placed it there did so carefully hoping to preserve it for better times. Perhaps, this was not done until the civil war period of the seventeenth century, when Wareham had a very puritan rector. The Reverend Thomas Chaplyn was installed when William Wake, the rector and a keen royalist, was removed. As Arne was from 1646 a daughter church of Holy Trinity in Wareham, perhaps it was at this time that the villagers at Arne removed their altar before Chaplyn could order its destruction himself.

The interior by then would have been whitewashed covering up all the paintings, and throughout the eighteenth and early nineteenth centuries, the churchwardens' accounts have several references to whitewashing. In 1831, for example, Charles Churchill was paid 13s 5 $^{1}/_{2}$d [68p] to do this.

Interior of Arne Church. Above the door on the right is part of the mediaeval wall mural.

As with the majority of Anglican buildings, by the nineteenth century Arne's church was probably looking the worst for wear. Little had been done over the centuries to keep it in good condition. Only repair jobs had been carried out, as when in 1838 George Shepherd was paid 6s [30p] for repairing some windows. Any work tended to be piecemeal, just keeping the structure from getting any worse. This was true of so many of our parish churches at this time. Hence, the Victorians, with their tremendous interest in old buildings, began a wholesale restoration. Sometimes this was far too drastic for later tastes, but they did save many of our buildings from falling down. Arne was no exception, and thanks to Lord Eldon, it was thoroughly restored; too much so for Sir Frederick Treves, writing in 1906: "The restorer has fallen upon it with little mercy." Later in the century the church architectural historian Fred Pitfield, writing in 1985, would be much more sympathetic.

Precise details of what was done by Lord Eldon are missing. The faculty which was obtained from the Bishop of Salisbury in 1856 authorising the work merely said that all the pews and fittings were to be taken out and replaced with "sufficient space for kneeling to be allotted to all." The only old seats that were kept were those reserved for the use of the parochial day school and for the Sunday school. At the same time a complete restoration of the fabric seems to have taken place. The Royal Commission on Historical

Monuments suggests that the buttresses may have been added at this time. All the work was paid for by Lord Eldon.

Services were held every Sunday in the afternoon just as they were two hundred years before. They more or less had to be, to fit in with those at Lady St. Mary's. In the 1920s it was Canon Blackett, tall, dignified, the respected rector of Wareham, who came down in his horse and trap. Once a month there was a Sunday morning service.

The bell for reminding the faithful that a service was about to begin was rung by Henry Gardner in the 1920s. Not everyone came. Usually about a dozen turned up, but spread out they gave the impression of a fuller church. Miss Lucas was the organist. She and her brother were very musical. He lived at 51 North Street, Wareham, where he sold pianos. He also went around the area tuning them. Every Sunday, Fred Hibbs, the baker near the station, who also ran the Post Office, brought Miss Lucas down to Arne. The instrument she played on was by the 'twenties about eighty years old. It had been given to Arne by the Countess of Eldon in 1842.

To produce any sound, organs of that period needed someone to pump them by hand. It was a wearisome job, and doubtless, a thankless one as well. This was another duty performed by Henry Gardner, but as he got older, he found it more and more arduous, and sometimes the sound coming from the pipes faded away when he grew tired and gave up. George Holland took over this job as well as the bell ringing.

It was upon this organ that Bob Dorey and his friends played when they came over from the estate yard at Encombe to do any repair work in the village, such as floorboards and roofs. Bob was one of the carpenters, and when they had a job at Arne he had to leave his house by 6.30 in the morning to load up his bike with the wood he needed. The larger pieces came by lorry. After a hard morning's work, they had their lunch quickly so they could have half an hour or so playing a tune on the organ.

Before the service started, the children who made up the little choir came to rehearse with Miss Lucas the hymns to be used. Later, Phyl Candy took over this, and the children, about nine of them, went down to the farm to practice on Friday evenings. The tradition of having a choir may not have been that old at Arne. The first mention in the churchwardens' accounts of music being specially purchased for services occurs in 1899, when music for Christmas was bought. The following year more sheet music was purchased. From this it could be deduced that there was no choir before 1899. On the other hand, Mrs. James Lucas, a farmer's wife in the village had been making surplices in 1837. Were they for the rector to wear when he came down instead of bringing his own from Wareham, or was there already a choir? If the latter, then the music purchased in 1899 was to supplement the tunes in the hymn book.

Whether the choir started in 1899 or were being supplied with new music were both developments which fitted in with what was happening elsewhere. The Victorian period saw all over the country an attempt to bring back a little colour into Anglican services, colour which many thought had been taken out at the Reformation, and so elsewhere church ornaments were brought back and choirs robed, instead of remaining in their day-to-day outfits. At Arne, in 1882, the churchwardens had paid for candles for the altar. This is the first time in the accounts that these are mentioned. The following year more were purchased for the Harvest Thanksgiving. Mrs. James Lucas when she was making the surplices also made some materials that had been specially bought for the purpose into altar cloths, a pulpit cushion and a cloth for the reading desk.

Phyl's mother used to arrange the flowers in the church, a duty she enjoyed for thirty-six years, until she was too ill to do it. Then, her daughter, Phyl, took over. Easter was, and still is, a very important occasion for flowers, and the primroses for this came from Encombe Woods, which were a mass of yellow at this time. The men used to go with scythes and cut them, and put them into a sack which they carried across to Arne. Here, Phyl, and any of the children who wanted to help, sorted them into bunches, with each bunch having three primrose leaves. Then, they were put into the little glass pots that Shippam's used to put their pastes in. These were set down in beds of moss, pulled up to hide the glass jars, so the little interior of the church was filled with green and yellow.

Harvest provided another opportunity to bring in a mass of flowers. It was helping with these that Dorrie Churchill and her sister remember. At Christmas, it was evergreens, red berried holly, ivy, and yew branches, that were cut down to decorate the interior.

Events much anticipated by the children were the magic lantern shows that were held in the church, during which they joined in singing hymns.

For the first four decades of this century, George Candy was one of the churchwardens. In fact he had been appointed in 1892, two years before he actually came to take up residence. He was appointed because he was likely to be a prominent villager, and in this he is typical of the other churchwardens who served in the nineteenth and twentieth centuries. They were all important farmers. Richard Talbot was churchwarden between 1802 and 1823, keeping the parish accounts. He ran Church Farm. Hezekiah Talbot took over from him and was churchwarden until 1830. James Boyt of Slepe Farm occupied the position between 1834 and 1838. Other holders of the office, whose names occur in the accounts, though the book is missing for 1847 to 1854, include Joseph Boyt of Arne Farm, between 1845 and 1854; George Grant of Slepe Farm, 1854 to 1887; and Charles Smith of Arne Farm, in 1882.

George Candy was not typical of these men in one respect. He remained churchwarden for fifty years, which was certainly a record for Arne. In April 1941, the Bishop of Salisbury recognised this and sent him a letter of congratulations. "Your record can scarcely be surpassed anywhere," he wrote, "and I write as your bishop to express my thanks and appreciation for your half century of devoted service to our Lord and his Church." It was a letter George felt very honoured to receive.

Although everyone might not go to the services regularly, they did come for the Christmas and Easter services, and most villagers brought their babies here to be christened. When they grew up, they came to be married here. The records at Dorchester show that during the nineteenth century, there were usually about two weddings a month here. 1851 and 1852 both saw three marriages, as did 1870, 1881 and 1897, while 1872 produced a record of four weddings, so did 1899.

One unusual wedding in 1918 was that of Albert Owen, a 35-year-old serving soldier. He married Margaret Davies-Burton, who gave her address as Arne, but she is not a name that people today remember, so perhaps she was a friend of the Woods and staying at Arne House. What made the marriage interesting in village history is that her fiance was serving with the Australian Imperial Force. He was a lieutenant with them. The Australian presence is well remembered in Wareham, so perhaps he was stationed there.

One of the great social events of village life was the wedding of George Candy's elder daughter, Vera, in 1925. As he was arguably the most important man living in the village, the marriage of his daughter would be an occasion. Her bridegroom was a 25-year-old engineer from Birmingham, Reginald Hockley. Perhaps, at that time it was not a name that most locals would have known, but he was to become extremely important in the world of advertising and marketing of technical products to engineering and industrial firms. With the outbreak of war in 1939, his experience and know-how made him a key figure in the British war effort at home producing machinery and equipment for the war, for which he was promoted to the rank of Major, and after the war, his continued service earnt him the O.B.E. and other awards. But, of course, in 1925, all this was undreamed of. He was, if the villagers enquired, an extremely dynamic young engineer who would probably do well for himself. Phyl and her friend were bridesmaids. Phyl was in pink and the friend in Air Force blue. It was a great occasion for the village and everyone was invited back to sample the beef which had been boiled in the great copper there.

Much later on, at the beginning of what became the Second World War, John Johnson was another member of the armed forces who was married here. He was from Surrey. His bride was Rosemary Morgan, who was at Admiralty House in Wareham. The last wedding before the Blitz was that of Anderson Colin Edwards, a civil servant, who married Juliet Wilson, the daughter of one of Wareham's surgeons.

Sources
Dorrie Churchill; Harry Clark; Bob Dorey; Phyl Marsh.
St. Nicholas's Church; Churchwardens' Accounts, D.C.R.O., PE ARN CW1 (1802-1911).
Parish Registers, D.C.R.O., PE ARN.
Royal Commission on Historical Monuments, *An Inventory of Historical Monuments in the County of Dorset*, vol. 2, 1970.
Sir Frederick Treves, *The Highways and Byways of Dorset*, 1906.
F. P. Pitfield, *Purbeck Parish Churches*, Dorset Publishing Company, 1985.
Letter to George Candy from The Bishop of Salisbury.

Drawn by the Lady Katharine Scott.

Arne Chapel. AD. 1858.

VII

Visitors

For a village that had no road passing through, but only a dead-end track down to the harbour, Arne had in the first half of the twentieth century a surprisingly large number of visitors. True, for many of its own women a walk into Wareham was as far as they could go, but the village attracted people from outside. Some came as friends and acquaintances of the villagers, especially of the Candys. Many for example journeyed here for one of George Candy's many shooting parties. Others came on holidays, and finding it to their liking kept on returning. Only a few found it so isolated that they never came back.

The Woods were one of the families who returned year after year for their holidays. They came from London, where Trevor Wood was a solicitor, but they fell in love with the area and returned every summer thereafter, until the war in 1939 put a stop to it. They always came down by train and were met at Wareham Station by Ford the taximan. He ran the garage just below St. Martin's Church. Armed with only what luggage they could carry, they clambered into the car and set off.

Joan Sturdy, who was one of the Wood's children, still remembers the excitement of that journey; "the absolute thrill of turning up Nutcrack Lane" in Stoborough. For a child from London used to smooth road surfaces, the roughness of the unmade-up lane served only to stimulate even more anticipation of the wonderful days ahead. "It always seemed that the gorse was in full flower. The smell of gorse was absolutely lovely as we jolted along the lane to Arne," she recalls.

Their destination was Arne House, which they rented each summer from Lord Eldon. It had been at one time just his lordship's hunting lodge, but it was now large enough for Mr. and Mrs. Wood and their five children, four girls and a boy, with its five bedrooms, sitting room, dining room and kitchen. They brought with them their cook and their nanny. The other servant, a house parlourmaid, they hired in the village.

The house was also large enough for them to have friends down to stay. One of those who did was their great uncle who collected wild flowers. He was in his element just roaming around the area discovering flowers and the different varieties of heather that grew on the commons of the Isle of Purbeck.

When the taxi drew up in the village, there was no drive for it to convey them right up to the front door. It therefore stopped by the church, and the family had to walk up through the woods. This, no doubt, for the children was magical and added to their excitement.

For Joan and her brother, Peter, Arne was very special. They had the freedom that they could never have in London and they went on lots of picnics. But it was their mother who added to the place's enchantment. She was a very enterprising and forward looking woman. She keenly took up the governess's suggestion that Arne was the perfect place for the children to learn to sail. Not that she had any knowledge of sailing, and perhaps at first she did not exactly relish the idea, but she was persuaded by the enthusiasm of the governess, and she agreed. She even accompanied the governess on a visit to Poole where they bought a boat, and came back with it to Shipstal, all across the harbour!

She got one of the Orchards, who as fishermen were well acquainted with the channels, the tides, and the waters of Poole Harbour, to go out with her two elder children, Joan and Peter, and their governess. Under his guidance, they not only learned to sail but they came to know all about the waters of Poole Harbour. Their first boat was a 16 ft cutter, "nice and safe," recalls Joan. It did not have a life-belt, but they always towed a dingy behind just in case, and they never ventured out of sight of land.

Both children took to this new hobby enthusiastically and it became their chief occupation. Although neither of their parents could swim — in London there was never any need to do so — their children did learn, and by the age of twelve Joan had become a reasonably good swimmer. As her brother grew older, he became a very keen sailor, joined the Parkstone Yacht Club, had his own boat, and did a lot of racing. All this because his mother had not vetoed the governess's suggestion.

Tennis was another popular activity with the family, and her father had a court constructed on what is now the village car park. It was one of the few pieces of fairly flat land near the House, even though it meant crossing the road to get to it. Phyl Candy was a frequent player there.

Mrs. Wood was also a keen gardener and turned the area around the house into an attractive garden.

The family were at Arne when the First World War ended, and Joan remembers that she and her brother made paper Union Jacks and went down to Shipstal waving them. Later, when their father came home from the war, they waited for him at the House until the excitement was too great and they began to walk along the road looking for him, waving their flags.

For the Woods, Arne was always a wonderful place, "a happy place" and a complete change from London. The other event that sticks in Joan's recollections is the occasion of own marriage with Donald Sturdy in 1939.

She had wanted to be married in Arne Church, but that was too small for all the friends and relatives on both sides. Lady St. Mary's at Wareham had to be used. Still, Arne House was used for the reception, in spite of an outspoken friend of her mother's who exclaimed "Really, Dorothea, I can't think of a house in the whole British Kingdom worse suited for a wedding reception than Arne, dripping laurels on one side, and slippery wet steps on the other!"

Before the Woods's time, Arne House had been occupied more or less as a residence by the Pinney brothers — Thomas and Richard. They were clay merchants, who came to the village to live and made their mark on the area. Indeed, in 1907 Richard Pinney, "Uncle Dicky" to Phyl Candy, is described in *Kelly's Directory* of that year as a J. P., and five years earlier he had been re-elected as a churchwarden for Arne. His wife was one of the school managers. His nephew, Frank Pinney Longmire, used to be sent down from Cumberland, where his parents lived, to spend his summer holidays with his uncle, and naturally since his uncle was a very keen sailor, young Frank learnt to sail on his uncle's boat which he kept down at Shipstal. "Uncle Dicky" got Jesse Baker from Poole to come and teach the lad. Later, in the 1930s, his daughter came to stay. "My memories of Arne in the 'thirties are of cockling and picnicking there, where we were the only people," she now recalls.

Another set of visitors who came regularly were the scouts. Every year large numbers of them came from different parts of the country to camp here. Many came from Wimborne. Some came from Salisbury. Others came from London, and on one occasion there was even a group from Belgium. They all had to get permission from Mr. Candy, who rented the land they wanted to camp on. A phone call, a letter to him, usually brought a favourable answer. He supplied their drinking water, and in return they would help beat out a heathfire, if one occurred.

It was the Wimborne Scouts whom Phyl Marsh still remembers. Under their scoutmasters, Stan James, who was also a keen photographer, and Jack Hart, they came camping in the fields just below the farm. Bill Tapper, their chairman, sometimes accompanied them. He later became mayor of Wimborne. Like many others, set up in the wake of Robert Baden-Powell's first scouting camp on Purbeck's Brownsea Island in 1908, the troop was twenty-five years old in 1933, and they returned to Arne for their camp until the war. Of course, the Candys were always invited along to their camp fire.

It was during one of their visits that perhaps one of the most important events for scouting in the area took place, important for both the troop and for the village. Mrs. Phoebe Fenn chose the village church for her marriage in 1934 with Mr. George Bowes, the scoutmaster. She was the widow of the vicar of Dawlish in Devon. George was also from Devon. The night before her wedding, his bride and her niece were invited to stay with the Candys. After the ceremony, a troop of scouts formed a guard of honour as they came out of the little church, and then pulled their car down the hill to the reception at the camp.

The 10th North London troop also came, with their Assistant Scout Master, Eddie Blow. He remembers that one of the fishermen down at Shipstal used to lend them his longboat for outings round Brownsea Island. Among those who came were Fred Zimmerman, Norman Sidwell, Bob and Vic Hooper, and Sid Dietman.

George Bowes married Phoebe Fenn in Arne Church.

Crusaders were another group who came. Betty Petty's brother belonged to the Parkstone and Canford Cliffs Branch, and he and his friends acted as hosts at their own expense to two groups of underprivileged boys from the London area. This holiday was arranged by the London Branch, and each

Pulling the wedding car from the Church (top left), beside Arne Farm, on the way to the reception at the scout camp.

Saluting the flag, at Arne, are the 10th Salisbury Scouts.

group stayed a fortnight. During the two weeks before the boys arrived, the local crusaders used to have their own camp. It was part holiday and part training and preparation for their guests from London. Dr. Morgan Williams, who was later well-known as a surgeon at Poole Hospital, and Dr. Risk, who was a general practitioner at Canford Cliffs, used to be responsible for the Dorset side of these arrangements.

The 1st Poole Sea Scouts came to Arne in the 1920s and continued to come right up until the war. All they had to do was just to sail across the harbour in their boat. This was the *Scout*. Later, it was replaced by the

Mansel-Pleydell, named for the local benefactor from a well-known Dorset family. To the local lads, this boat was always the *Whaler*. They remember it as

Three Wimborne Scouts, camping at Arne.

having "nice lines", but it was difficult to row and was therefore rather slow. Later, the *Sharpy* — "an awful looking thing!" — was another of their boats.

Sometimes the lads came to camp, but more often they just sailed across and tied up to the pontoon at Shipstal and had one of Mrs. Orchard's cream teas — "marvellous cream teas!" — which appealed to hungry teenagers as they did to many other visitors. They still conjure up a mouth-watering feast in the minds of many older people, scouts and other visitors.

When the lads, inspired by one of their number, Arthur "Dick" Burden, built their own kayaks, seven in all, they could shoot across to Shipstal much more quickly than under sail. Each kayak carried two scouts, and the lads often went in them all over the harbour, even taking their girlfriends with them on occasions.

It was not difficult to come over to Shipstal in them. They would haul them up on the shore and go rambling inland in the sure knowledge that the kayaks would still be there on their return. For a camping holiday, the boat might have to do two trips to carry all the equipment they needed, which then had to be manually carried the half mile or so up from the beach to the camp site. Roy Dean still remembers trundling up with the heavy water-casks, but it was worth it. "We loved it," said Jack Fancy. Their site was usually one on the left of the track as they came up from Shipstal in a

Global warming also had its impact in the mid-1930s, with scoutmaster George Bowes (right) from Devon, and Jack Hart (centre), on the parched lake-bed beside Froxen Copse.

A party of 1st Wimborne Scouts being drilled by Jack Hart,
with their scoutmaster, Stan James, second from right

clearing. A little further off the track was a pool and the boys went across to it for their morning wash. "It was cold," remarked Roy. Sometimes, they went up the hill nearer the village and camped there, again on the left. Roy also remembered staying down in the valley on the right. It was while they were camping there that they were caught in a thunderstorm.

Charlie Dunford was in charge of the boys, and Arthur Brown was their scoutmaster. Charlie Moon often came with them in the early days. To be

Colour party of scouts between the Church (left) and Arne Farm
for the Bowes-Fenn wedding in 1934.

1st Poole Sea Scouts, at Shipstal Point in 1933. Left to right are two unidentified boys, Vic Rodgers (hatted); Harold Turner, Arthur Burden, George Beveridge, Roy Dean, two unidentified, Sid Woodland, two more unidentified and Don Masters steering.

taken for a ride in his open-topped little sports car was a tremendous thrill at a time when a car was still a novelty. He used to take them all over the place. He drove Jack Fancy to a boxing tournament at Bryanston in it, much to the teenager's delight. He also owned a boat, *Luna*, which was a dolphin class sailing dingy. The scouts always referred to her as the *Mooney*, and

A party of Belgian scouts arriving at Arne, between the School (left) and the Church.

Dennis and his friend, Roy Dean, used to crew for him. It was a bitter blow for them all when Charlie was killed, in a motoring accident, not long after Roy joined the scouts in 1934.

Most of the scouts were Poole lads, living not far from their meeting place in Skinner Street Congregational Chapel. Not far away, in Green Lane was their den, a cosy, nice place, with a fireplace and small snooker table. Dennis, Jack and Roy were all friends who lived near the lifeboat station at the far end of the Quay.

While they were at Arne, they took part in all kinds of scouting activities, hiking, tracking, training for their proficiency badges, and camp fires, as well as swimming down at Shipstal, though they seem to recall that there was a lot more sand down there at that time than there is today. They did not swim out very far — just around the pontoon — perhaps because it was too muddy. So Roy's swim over to Long Island and back was something of an event. Inshore enjoyments included searches for cockles.

One problem that many of the Poole lads faced was that they had paper-rounds at Looker's, the newsagents and booksellers in the High Street, and they could not afford to have a holiday while they were camping, so each day their boat had to sail across the harbour, wait for them to complete their rounds, and bring them back to Arne again. In this they must have been unique among the scouts who camped at Arne.

Some visitors did not come from as far away as most of the scouts. Joan Green only came down from Ridge. At first she came with her father, "Oily" Green, the paraffin man. His sister kept the village post office at Stoborough, which had its half-day closing on a Thursday, the same as her father, so both families used to pile into her father's van and come down to Arne and have a picnic and a paddle at Shipstal, never a swim! When she grew older, Joan could come on her bike.

For her friend, Eva Gover, it was her father's rowing boat that brought them down the river from Ridge. They usually went to Russel Quay and often brought their tent with them so they could camp over a weekend. "Dad would find a spot with fresh water in the sand and scoop it out and you'd get fresh water," she recalls.

Eva also came eel-bobbing with a line and a piece of string and a bob of worms. "You had a bobbing-needle. You'd thread the worms on, usually wool. We loved doing that, digging up worms and threading them on." Both now remember that whenever they were here, there were very few other people, so they had the whole beach at Shipstal or at Russel Quay all to themselves.

In addition there were some people who just passed through the village. Young Harry Clark and his brother were such a pair. They came through with their nursemaid on their way down to Shipstal, where one of the Orchard family would row them across to Long Island for a holiday.

Another who came this way was the international flying celebrity, Amy Johnson. She often stayed at Bournemouth, and while she was there she would pay a visit to her friends on the island. She would leave her car by the church and call in at the Candys' until the Orchards were ready to row her across.

There were other visitors who came, but they tended to come to stay, at least for a number of years, and so could be classified as semi-residents. Obviously, the ladies who came as schoolmistresses fall into this category. For example, Georgina Hockley, who was at the schoolhouse between 1911 and 1912. Did she have with her her two sons, who were growing from boys to teenagers? We assume she did. One of her boys was later to become Major General Anthony Hockley, an important figure in Britain's next war effort from 1939 onwards. Her other son, Reginald, went into engineering. Was it while they were at the schoolhouse that the young Vera Candy came to know Reginald, whom she was to marry in 1925?

When the school finally closed in 1922, the house was let and this brought in more semi-permanent residents. Mr. and Mrs. Romsey were the first. They were a retired couple. Then, Mrs. Ryder had the lease for a short time. After this, came Mrs. Kitchin, or at least that was how she described herself to the villagers. She had not been here long with her husband before Bert Candy, Phyl's brother, discovered her importance. It came about because he was a keen stamp collector, and, finding this out, Mrs. Kitchin once gave him an envelope full of stamps that she had saved for him. On returning home and showing the stamps to his mother, they both noticed the inscription on the envelope: "The Hon. Mrs. Kitchin". Mrs. Candy remarked on this when she next met the lady.

"Ssssh!,", came the reply, "I love to go round to talk to the village people, and they'd curl up if they knew that!"

The Candys did not let on.

The Honourable Mrs. Kitchin was in fact one of four daughters of the first Baron Ilkeston, Balthazar William Foster, who had a very distinguished medical career in late Victorian England and entered politics as the Liberal member for Chester and then for Derby. Prime Minister Asquith created him Baron Ilkeston during the constitutional struggle with the House of Lords in 1910.

His daughter, Margaret, at the age of twenty married Brook Taylor Kitchin. *Burke's Peerage* of 1931 described him as "the architect" of the Local Government Board, which Gladstone had created in 1871 to take over the work of looking after the poor. He was thus a highly suitable husband for the

The Hon. Mrs. Margaret Kitchin came to live in the Schoolhouse at Arne in 1941. She was Lord Ilkeston's daughter.

daughter of a fellow Liberal, especially since his father was a rising personality in the Anglican Church. He was eventually appointed Dean of Durham Cathedral in 1894, a position he held until his death in 1912. All this, of course, happened long before Brook and Margaret came to Arne.

When they did so, they had the schoolhouse enlarged and toilets put in. A bedroom was made over the old classroom. Their daughter, Nancy, used to come down and stay, sometimes bringing with her her daughter, Jill. Occasionally, Jill's husband came with them. He was Brian Horrocks, who became Lieutenant-General Horrocks, of Arnhem mayhem and fame. He was another very important person who in the 1930s had connections with Arne.

With the advent of war in 1939 Mrs. Kitchin gave up the house here and moved back to Wimbledon, where she had come from. Her husband, Brook, died in June 1940, and in his memory she presented Arne church with a "new" altar rail. It was new only to Arne, for the rail was about two hundred years old! Brook Kitchin's brother was an architect in Winchester, and the old rail had been taken out of a church there. He gave it to his brother's family, and that is how Arne came to have such an interesting altar rail.

Mr. Bucknell was another of these semi-permanent visitors. He lived on his yacht which he moored just south of Shipstal. He was there for a number of

Arne hermit Mr. Bucknell lived on a yacht, moored in the creek opposite Long Island.

years in the 'thirties. One of the lifeboats from the liner *Majestic* served as his storehouse, where he kept all his things. It was beached a little way up on the shore. The Candys did not know him well, but they learnt that his father had been at one time an architect in Algiers, and that he had two sisters, one of whom lived in a convent at Stroud in Gloucestershire.

Although he kept himself to himself, he used to come up to the farmhouse for tea regularly twice a week, and it was arranged that if he failed to turn up, one of the Candys would go down to see if he was alright. One Friday in the early part of the war, he did not come, so Phyl went down with the keeper's niece to see what was the matter. She had a hard job to get on board, but when she did manage it, she found the old boy had had a stroke and could not speak. While Phyl stayed with him, the keeper's niece ran back to the farm to raise the alarm, and George Candy sent down the horse and cart. The troops up at the camp came down with a stretcher, and they managed to get him into Wareham to Christmas Close, the successor to the Workhouse, but he did not survive long. Then, the Candys had to get rid of his things, but his yacht and the lifeboat sold for almost nothing, it being wartime.

By contrast, some only paid a fleeting visit here. Several came across the harbour and landed at Shipstal just to sample Mrs. Orchard's cream teas, while an even briefer stop was made by some of those who came with the "Beating of the Bounds", a ceremony designed to proclaim the boundary between Poole and Wareham. This ancient ceremony had lapsed but was revived in 1921 and became a popular annual event until the next war, and as such was eagerly looked forward to by the village children. Dorrie and her sister loved to get up on the hill at the cranery and watch the procession of gaily decorated boats as they passed and re-passed during the ceremony.

First, the fleet of ships came sailing up the Wareham Channel from Poole

and stopped at Russel Quay. Here, a small party from Poole landed and visited the boundary stone there. Once more back on board, the procession sailed on up river to Wareham, where its mayor and his friends were welcomed board, and then the whole procession sailed back down river this time to stop at Shipstal, where the landing party came ashore.

One of the lifeboats from the liner Majestic,
where Mr. Bucknell stored his provisions at Shipstal Point.

In 1923, this was a very important occasion, more so than usual. Lord
Eldon wanted to hand over formally a deed making the footpath down to
Shipstal a public right of way. Accordingly a luncheon had been arranged for
the important guests on the grass so his agent could perform the ceremony

Beating the Bounds of Poole Harbour, off Shipstal Point, on 11 August 1937.
The pontoon was erected for the occasion.

The Mayors of Poole and Wareham at the Beating the Bounds ceremony.

and hand over the deed. In return for this concession, the public right of way down to Russel Quay was cancelled and the track closed.

Another fleeting visitor during the 1930s was the watercolour artist, A. H. Berens. He lived at "Full Stop" in Studland, and Phyl Candy was asked over on several occasions. She remembers a carved wooden bear, or lion, holding up the main beam of the cottage, and there were several Siamese cats about the place. He was usually accompanied by his pupil, Elizabeth Armsden. After one of their visits to Arne, she composed a charming coloured etching of the fishermen down at Shipstal.

Sources

Again, much of this chapter is based on the memories of Dorrie Churchill, Phyl Marsh, and Joan Sturdy.

The author is also very grateful to Roy Dean, Jack Fancy and Dennis Proudley, all former Sea Scouts of Poole; to Mrs. Betty Pettey for the information about her brother; to Eddie Blow, Fred Zimmerman, and R. J. Judge, all former London Scouts; and to Joan Jacobs; Eva Biles; H. J. S. Clark; Judith Cooper; to A. W. Potter, Research Assistant with The Royal Academy of Arts, London; and to the more than helpful staff of Keele University Library in Staffordshire.

Rodney Legg, *Literary Dorset,* 1990.

Poole and East Dorset Herald Files, Poole Library.

Who Was Who, 1897-1915.

The last peacetime shoot at Arne, in 1939, with keeper Cyril Ford and son Don in the centre.

Owen Stevens (kneeling) with other shooters including the Commanding Officer at Arne Camp and a restaurant owner from Bournemouth.

VIII
Wartime

The coming of war in 1939 was to change Arne completely, but this was far from being obvious at the outset. To the military authorities, however, the area was a site of outstanding strategic importance. The small hills around the village commanded superb views over the harbour, and just across the water was the vital Royal Naval Cordite Factory at Holton Heath, which made the propellant for the Navy's shells and would be a sure target for any enemy action. Even before the war, during the Munich crisis, the Germans had been surveying the area, examining its potential. Nina Bishop recalls an incident in the summer of 1938, when she was swimming at Shell Bay and saw a large Zeppelin hovering overhead. She learnt afterwards from an uncle who worked at Holton Heath that the airship had travelled all along the coast and was probably taking pictures of all the naval and military installations it came across. For that reason, no one had been allowed above ground at Holton Heath during the whole day, until the Zeppelin had moved far away.

Because of its strategic importance, Arne was chosen as the site for four heavy artillery guns [SY 969 882]. There was, in addition, a fifth gun near the track down to Shipstal [SY 984 884]. This was a light artillery gun. Close by was a searchlight, though this was later in 1941 moved to another site elsewhere, where it was felt it would be more useful. A further gun was mounted on the hill to the west of Ridge nearer to Wareham, and there was decoy near Bank Gate in a field belonging to Slepe Farm. This was to play an important part in the story of Arne during these years. Locals knew very little about it. A sentry box, big enough for two soldiers to stay in, and a tank stood near-by, but Reg Smith admits that the villagers never cottoned on to it being a decoy. "We thought it was an experiment or something."

All the guns needed manning twenty-four hours a day, so a small camp was built on the hill to the west of the church on open heathland. Since the Forestry Commission have taken over the area after the war, it has changed out of all recognition. They planted hundreds of trees. In 1939, it was open countryside, though Phyl Candy remembers that a few trees had to be cut down to make way for the camp. Don Gilbert was among the first soldiers to be drafted here early in August 1939. He recalls digging out the gunpits and the command post and filling countless sandbags to protect the site. This was for a naval gun, a Predictor and a Height Finder. At first the soldiers slept in bell tents, but not for long. They were soon replaced by wooden huts, which arrived in sections from a Wareham contractor

The Cookhouse at Arne Camp. Pictured left to right are an unidentified man, Gunner Jim Sharp, Gunner Dower, and Cook Pascoe.

and were put up by the soldiers themselves. Jim Hearmon who came in October of the same year remembers only these wooden huts; two or three for the men, and a few more for the officers. A cookhouse, canteen, stores hut, toilet, washhouse, and an ammunition store made up the other buildings on the top of the hill. All were surrounded with a fence, with a guard hut positioned at the gate where the track from the village came up. With so many men in, the camp needed a special pipe for its water supply, and so one was installed to bring it from the fresh water pools down at Russel Quay. A little pump was put in to force the water up to the camp.

Whether tents or huts, it was home to about forty men of the 56th Heavy Anti-Aircraft Regiment of the Royal Artillery. The first men came from Cornwall, from Helston, Truro and Redruth, like Don Gilbert. With him were his fellow soldiers, Lieutenant George Berriman, Sergeants Short and English, Brigadier Kemp, Gunners Clifton, Hoskins, Harris, Hart and Ratallack to name a few; and, of course, his friend, Len Oliver. They were joined by others from Camborne, also in Cornwall, and from South Wales, and later from London and the North. At the outset of the war, the 56th H.A.A. had been the 1st Monmouths, a territorial regiment, but had now been re-organised. Many must have found the camp, as another arrival, Ron Kiddle, did, "a very isolated place."

On Jim Hearmon, it made a deep impression. "I was posted to Arne as a newly commissioned second lieutenant. I arrived in the dusk on a very wet October day, and, as I alighted from the truck, it seemed to me that the whole place was surrounded by water. However the next day the sun shone, and I realised two things; firstly, that it was a textbook gun position, with an all round field of fire down to minimum elevation; secondly, that it was a very beautiful spot, with the vast sweep of heath and water, the Purbeck Hills away to the south and the ruins of Corfe Castle — the known distance marker which we used to check and adjust over our range finder."

In this attractive setting, life at the camp was very routine, the constant maintenance of the guns, the filling of sandbags, and, of course, the frequently exhausting fatigues. For most of the time, there was little excitement or danger.

So the men had time to look around, and other things captured their imagination. Jim Hearmon recalls the thrill of seeing Sunderland and Catalina flying boats taking off or coming in to land on the harbour.

For Phyl Candy, too, these planes were exciting. "There used to be three of them," she recalls, "and they were wonderful. We looked forward to seeing them. They used to come over two or three times a day, and circle around from Poole Harbour."

With Dunkirk, and the fall of France in May 1940, the German invasion seemed imminent. The long dark nights of the winter that followed brought

Outdoor catering on Arne Heath in August 1939. The gunners are Hoskins, Jack Downing, Retallack, Williams, Percy Pethick, and person unknown.

Gunners and bell-tents of the first military encampment on Arne Heath.
Left to right are Jim Kemp, Jack Williams, Jim Coombe, Charlie Wearne and Jack Pascoe.

Battery Observation Post on Arne Heath, with predictor, height-finder and sight-ranging
instruments. Len Oliver is using the height-finder and Don Gilbert is
observing with binoculars.

night after night of noise of Germen bombers as they flew over. "We were out every night firing at German planes," recollects Ron Kiddle. Arne seemed to be on the flight path for many inland cities; Bristol, Cardiff, Swansea, Liverpool, and even Belfast.

"We always knew where they were heading for," Audrey Richards recalled. "If they went one way, they were going to Southampton. If they went straight across, they were off to the Midlands."

"They passed over us in long processions," said Jim Hearmon, "and again on their return, so we had some long nights on the guns."

It was then that the returning bombers tried to ditch any remaining bombs on board to lighten their weight as they struggled back across the Channel. There was so much activity during these nights that the guncrew had to be supplemented by men from the area headquarters at Lytchett Minster. Ron Kiddle was one of them. He was there for only a few months before he was recalled to Lytchett.

Occasionally, the Arne lads were able to shoot down a plane. It boosted their zeal and confidence when they were officially informed by the authorities that they had been "credited with the destruction of two planes, and a half share in another".

There were not many direct attacks on the station, but Jim Hearmon does recall one taking place in the spring of 1941. The target was the flying boats in the harbour, and the enemy planes swept in low. "None of the flak reached Arne, and the harbour defences put up a wonderful show of tracer," he writes. This attack appears to be an addition to those listed in Rodney Legg's *Dorset at War*.

Another incident Jim brought to mind was when a R.A.F. fighter crashed on the heath over towards Middlebere. The pilot bailed out, but afterwards the lads at Arne heard that the parachute had failed to open. This was probably the same one that Reg Smith saw come down. "We see it come in — a young laddie from Weymouth, Watson, I believe, about 20. Been on patrol on the Channel. A plane came in over Brownsea and Middlebere, with bits coming off him. We were on the hill. He came down in the bog."

This crash can certainly be dated using Rodney Legg's book to 28th November 1940, and the pilot was indeed Arthur Ray Watson of 152 Squadron in a Spitfire from R.A.F. Warmwell.

Dennis Coombes and his grandfather also saw the spitfire as it swept over Two Gates, crossed the marsh, turned, came back again, and then turned again, but this time it plunged upside down into the marsh. The nose went down about sixteen feet. He was doing about 100mph, estimates Dennis. The old man and the boy saw the pilot bail out just before the crash and open

Construction of a gun-pit on Arne Heath. Left to right are Lance-Bombadier Williams, person unknown, and Gunners J. Sharp, Fred Penaluna, and Jim Kemp.

his parachute within seconds. His grandfather told young Dennis to run back home to let his grannie know they were alright, while he went to see if he could help the pilot. This meant that he had to run down to the road, along it for a short distance and then back along the ridge of the hill. When he got there, he saw the airman on the cycle path of the old clay line from Norden to Middlebere. "His bones sticking out," the old chap told Dennis. "He was no more than 18."

Meanwhile Reg and Fred Battrick had arrived at the scene of the crash. They could still hear the engine "tissing".

"We're not safe here," said Reg in alarm. "So we got away and found the pilot ... He'd bailed out, but his parachute never opened — not really high enough. Then the police arrived and took the body away."

Sometimes the alert would go at the camp and the men leapt into action, only to find that nothing happened. The enemy planes had evidently gone elsewhere. During the long light summer months attack was less likely, but the guns still had to be manned. The hours seemed to crawl by.

The often monotonous routine at the camp was occasionally relieved by a visit to Holton Heath, for a bath, or to help at the cordite factory there. This was no light escape. It was, as Don Gilbert remembers, very exhausting. They had to load the ammunition onto trains for other parts of the United Kingdom. A haulier from Wareham came with his truck to transport the men there and bring them back afterwards.

Lance-Bombadier Williams in action, elevating the barrel in gun-laying on Arne Heath.
Note the ammunition boxes and shells stacked behind him.

Heath fires provided another break, perhaps a highly dangerous one, from camp. If a fire broke out, messages were sent up to the camp for help, but usually only two or three men could be spared from the essential, if dull, work. The efforts of those who were sent were very gratefully received by the villagers, who would afterwards provide some beer money at the canteen.

Frequently, the locals were able to help the soldiers. Lewis Gover, from Ridge, was one who did. With his gun in his hand and his dog at his side, he was a common sight about the heathland in those days. He provided the camp with fresh rabbits, which he left outside the fence, covered over, for the men to retrieve later. It first started when some soldiers came and asked him to get them some rabbits. "But, for Christ sake, take their guts out!" they pleaded.

Even the officers got to know of his "war efforts."

He was stopped one night by an astounded officer who demanded, "Who the hell are you?"

Gover shouted back "Keep your bloody great mouth shut, and I'll tell you in a minute!"

Fortunately, the officer recognised the voice as that of the local benefactor.

The Candys also helped whenever possible to make life a little more comfortable for the lads on the hill. They had large numbers of poultry, so

Salvaging a break-away barrage balloon in 1940. Left to right are Gunner Williams, Gunner Dyke, Gunner Bond, Gunner Williams, Sergeant English, Gunner Nicholas, an unknown Gunner, and a local contractor.

they were able to send up to the troops plenty of eggs. The cook would let the men have a little bit of fat, and they could have egg and toast, or fried egg, or scrambled egg for their supper.

The Smiths helped by looking after some of the soldiers' wives when they came down to visit their husbands. Ron Kiddle's wife, Gladys, was made very welcome and looked after very well indeed. For this they were very grateful. Their young son could play with the Smith's lad, Royston. This arrangement enabled Ron to spend some time with his wife and son, before going back for his spell of night duty.

Because of its isolation, and the shortage of staff on the site, the men found it very difficult to get away when they were off duty. The lucky ones might manage to cadge a lift on the lorry that came from Wareham with the rations. At the beginning of the war, the army did not have enough of its own vehicles, so a local haulier brought in the rations. He did not mind offering a ride to any soldier who was off duty and who wanted to get away. If anyone accepted and went as far as Wareham, he had to make his own way back again, but soldiers in those days did not think much about walking the four miles back to Arne in the dark.

Jim Hearmon writes, "Their return was heralded long before their arrived at the site. In the still of the night, they could be heard singing as they tramped along the heath road."

Don Gilbert was even luckier. His friend, Len Oliver, still had his own car, an Austin 10, and at weekends he would take as many as possible into Wareham. When the inside of the car was full, the lads held onto the outside. An afternoon meal at the tea shop in South Street, run by two old ladies, or just browsing in the shops, or a night out at their favourite pub, the Black Bear; these are what Don now remembers the local town for. Then, back to camp clinging to Len's car! To be back by midnight!

For those who had to remain back at camp, social life revolved around the canteen. Many happy hours were passed there drinking. On one occasion, the soldiers were astounded to receive a rocket from headquarters suggesting they spent too much time in the bar. The memo read; "Ack-Ack should not mean beer-beer!"

Sometimes parties were organised in the canteen. Phyl Candy was often invited to them. Jim Hearmon remembers a concert being put on by Lady Lees of Lytchett Manor. She played the violin. Another was put on by the E.N.S.A. team of Eric and Phyl Dean. She was a Miss Kent and lived at Norden on a farm. She played the piano, for Eric, who lived in Bournemouth, and used to dress for these concerts as a yokel in a smock. They were in much demand at the time.

But the event that still stick in Jim's mind was the dance that was held in the camp! When it was first discussed, the idea was greeted with great scepticism. After all where would they get the girls from? One of the N.C.O.s volunteered to hire a coach and bring some over from Poole. This raised many

"P" Section of the 165th Heavy Anti-Aircraft Regiment at Arne Camp.

an eyebrow, and one chap wanted to know whom he had worked for before he joined up. "Harrods!" came the proud answer. "The universal providers!" On the night of the dance, he certainly lived up to his former employer's motto. There were partners for all, and everyone had a marvellous time!

For thousands of girls up and down the country, war played havoc with their dreams for their wedding day, and Phyl Candy was no different. She could not have a big wedding with a large number of guests and a separate party for the villagers, as her sister had had. Instead, like many others, it had to be a fairly quiet occasion. Coupons and rationing had seen to that. Her husband to be, Fred Marsh, was the son of the farmer at Bestwell, near Wareham, and the time set for the ceremony, January 1940, saw Fred in France. He had volunteered at the outbreak of war, but was allowed leave to come home. As everyone supposed that Fred would be in battledress, Phyl was told white would not be suitable, so she suggested green. "The Marshes said they were superstitious about green, so I was married in a blue dress, with grey fur, and grey gloves, and grey shoes, and a little grey hat." It was not easy to collect such an outfit as everything was rationed and clothing coupons had to be surrendered for each new article. In the event, Fred was allowed to wear "civvies," a dark suit.

For many brides during the war years, it was getting the ingredients for the cake that proved as difficult as getting the wedding dress. However, for Phyl, this was not a problem. "Mr. Tweed, of Bennetts, the bakers in Wareham, said he would like to give me the wedding cake," which he did.

The biggest problem was whether the groom would make it. "Fred arrived the night before from France, with a temperature of 105!" His family were up all that night with him, and did not think he would see the service in the village church through, but with everyone's support the marriage went on. "We had a reception at home, and quite a lot of people came back. We were going to London, but he was so ill that his sister, Doris, and her husband, who lived in Christchurch, gave us the key to go down there and stay." Fred was later diagnosed as having double pneumonia and German measles, and it was eleven weeks before he could return to his outfit!

The officers at Arne Camp were luckier than many of the ordinary soldiers. The friendship, help and kindness of George Candy and his family during their stay at Arne remains a lasting memory. They used to come down to use the telephone, as the Candys had the only one in the village. While they waited for a call, which could last anything up to a couple of hours, to come through, a glass of home-brew would be offered.

Some came down to collect letters that were left there for them, or to pay for newspapers that Phyl used to order from Renee Burt in Wareham.

Twenty-one newspapers were ordered each day from the shop in North Street. In addition, Phyl managed to get four radios for use at the camp on a weekly rental. On other occasions, the lads came down to have a sing-song, play games and to stay for supper.

Christmases were a special time for the farm, and the Candys made the soldiers feel at home. Phyl remembers some Welsh lads really raising the roof with their carol singing, and on another Christmas Eve some former choir men from Cornwall singing very beautifully.

Arne made a lasting impression on the many young men who were sent here. Jim Hearmon probably summed it up very well. "For many of us, Arne was a rather special place, a lonely community tucked away on the heaths. Church, farm, cottage, old schoolhouse and Mrs. Marsh's flower garden opposite the farmhouse. Add sunshine, the sparkle of the surrounding waters and the smell of heather and gorse. It's something we shall always remember."

Don Gillbert also enjoyed his stay here. "Being a young soldier, life was full of adventure."

The coming of war and the presence of the army camp affected the villagers as well. Obviously, the threat of air-raids was very serious in 1939, and the government was at pains to point out the need for a shelter. For the Candys, this was to be the old cellar beneath their house. For Joan Green over at Ridge, it was a dug-out refuge at the top of their garden, sunk into the ground and covered with grass.

For her friend, Eva Gover, it was the big ditch around their garden. Today, looking back, she does not know what good it would have done if a bomb had fallen close-by, but at the time, they felt it got them out of the house. It could only be used in dry weather, so if it was raining, they stayed indoors.

Joan's family too did not bother much in the early days about using their shelter. Later, when her father was called up, her mother would always get up when the siren went at night and make Joan shelter under the dining room table. Later still, as her daughter got older, she refused even to leave her bed.

For Brian Hallett at Ridge Farm, the shelter was one his father made in the garden out of wood and galvanised tin. He found some old pews to put inside to make it more comfortable.

For Nancy Smith and her family at Slepe Farm, there was no special shelter. The authorities, it was surmised, did not think the farm would be attacked as it was too much of a landmark for planes. Whenever there was a raid on, they had to go into their sitting room and take refuge behind the heavy sandstone and mortar wall which kept back the hillside at the end of the room. It seemed very strong.

Her brother, Reg, down at Bank Gate in one of the three cottages there had an Anderson shelter in the garden.

But schoolgirl, Audrey Richards, did not want a shelter. For her, the excitement of a raid was too great and she often went out into the garden to see the searchlights' glare catch any planes overhead.

The only raid where Joan Green remembers being really frightened, was a daytime attack — "something as scary as that lives with you for ever! I don't remember the exact date, but it must have been during the school holiday. My gran, my mum's mother, was staying with us at the time. The bombers always came during this period early in the afternoon, and we were on their flight path, I think. On this particular day, we had finished lunch, and, because we still cooked on a double burner paraffin stove, on which we would sit an oven, it was usual for mum to have cakes ready to put in to cook once she had finished cooking lunch. It was a clear sunny afternoon."

This would appear to be the incident recorded by Rodney Legg in *Dorset Aviation Encyclopaedia* as occurring on 7th October 1940.

Joan continued: "The siren went and the bombers started coming over, and because the cakes were not quite cooked I was told to run up to the shelter, which was right at the top of the garden. For some reason, gran decided to stay with mum, and they were going to follow me up within five minutes or so. I was standing in the doorway of the shelter, watching for mum and gran, when I heard this awful screaching noise that a plane makes when it's out of control. Appearing over Harp Hill just behind me was a plane with black smoke pouring from one of its engines. The noise was deafening and frightening. I must have been rooted to the spot and I watched it making straight for our house! — or so it seemed to me at the time. In fact, it went over and crashed about a quarter of a mile out in the common, where it exploded, because it was still carrying all its bombs."

"Mum and gran came rushing up to see that I was alright. They had been equally rooted to the spot. It seems that they were just on their way up when the plane appeared, and their reaction was to get back into the house but they only managed to get to the door and just stood their waiting for the bang. I remember mum saying that it was possible to see the pilot because the plane was so low."

"There was very little left of either the plane or the pilot, and for many years there was a Purbeck stone cairn out on the common, on which sometimes there would be flowers."

Many years later when the common was turned back to agricultural use, the stone was removed. At the time, Joan felt only extremely relieved that nothing had happened to her mum or her gran, but "now as an adult it makes one think that it could have been a brave act on the part of the pilot to turn round and find an open space. He must have known that he would have no chance of surviving. I seem to recollect hearing that the rest of the crew had bailed out. Of course, had the worst scenario happened, and it had crashed on the buildings, there was a 500 gallon tank of paraffin in the store. That would have set up a good blaze, wouldn't it?"

Another raid Joan remembers again occurred when her gran was staying with them: "Every afternoon the siren went just as we were leaving school. On this occasion, gran came to meet me. As we were coming up the lane, over came the bombers, so we hurried along to get to Two Big Trees", two English elms, "where we could take cover. Just as we got into the ditch, a chauffeur-driven car pulled up, and a chauffeur opened the door to allow this rather posh, well-spoken — deaf — lady to join us in the ditch! Poor gran was very out of breathe from hurrying, but this woman kept telling gran not to panic because she was frightening the child (me!); but no amount of explaining would make her understand because she couldn't hear! The finale act in this episode was when mum appeared on her bike, still in her apron and equally out of breathe, rushing to make sure that gran and I were alright."

Fortunately, such close raids were fairly rare. One that could have been extremely dangerous for Phyl Candy was when she and Fred Marsh, her husband to be, were driving back to Arne. She had been across to Wareham Station to pick him up as he had spell of leave. They were on their way back through Ridge, when the siren went, and they saw a lone plane flying towards them dropping bombs! About five bombs in all, Phyl reckons. In panic, she stopped the car and Fred hurtled himself into the nearest ditch, but Phyl just stood by the side of her car. "I couldn't get my white coat dirty, could I?"

She recalls hearing a bomb drop into the clay not far from her, but fortunately it did not explode. After this, they got back into her car, and drove quickly home. This happened where the road crosses the narrow railway line that used to take clay down to the river at Ridge, and for all she knows the bomb is still there deep down in the clay.

At Arne, Phyl remembers another low-flying plane which frightened her. She was up in her bedroom one afternoon, looking out of the window. "The siren had gone. I heard this terrific noise coming. Henry Gardner happened to be in the yard. All of a sudden, I saw him run and get under a wagon." A plane was flying very low over the farmyard. "It was very frightening. It was level with the windows, and machine-gunning as well. Poor Henry!"

Nancy Smith still remembers standing in the kitchen at Slepe and seeing an aircraft flying so low it was almost on the ground. It was probably this one that her brother Reg saw and wished he had had a gun. He could, he thinks, have brought the plane down.

His brother, Jess, had that morning suggested that he, his father and Nancy could cope with the milking, if Reg preferred to get on with ploughing up Thirty Acres. Accordingly, Reg had set off on his bike. He got up as far as the Knap when he saw the plane flying low — so low that it was below the range of the guns on Arne Hill. It came up from Brownsea way and, as he stopped, Reg could see quite clearly the pilot's face. "He's looking down at me. I daren't wave lest he shoot me. He flew very low." The pilot managed not to crash but went on. A few minutes later, Reg heard the "wamp-wamp" as it came down in Swanage. It crashed into the bank by the station, killing the manager and wrecking the building.

This may be the same tragedy, recorded in Rodney Legg's *Dorset Aviation Encyclopaedia*, as that which took place on 17th August 1942 when the Westminster Bank in Swanage received a direct hit. Eight people were killed. Could this have been due to Reg's plane, or was it a completely different incident?

Planes were something they had to live with, as long as they were in the sky and at a distance. It was a constant topic of conversation for the bricklayers and the labourers working to rebuild the farm at Slepe. The dogfights and the antics of the planes overhead were compelling, but a plane hurling earthwards was something far more serious. On one occasion, Phyl

Peacetime picture, from June 1934, of the rickyard where the German aeroplane would frighten the life out of Henry Gardner (right), seen with Carter Roberts and Trixie.

counted 23 planes in the sky. A day or so later, she went for a walk along the footpath to Coombe. She was about halfway there when she saw something white in the bracken. "I did go and have a good look, but I realised it was a parachute, and I ran all the way back!"

Again, this was probably the same incident that Reg Smith remembers. He had been to Wareham market with his father and mother. On the way home, they noticed a string of enemy bombers flying towards the coast, coming from over Dorchester way. The Smiths thought they might have been attacking Exeter or Plymouth. They also saw two spitfires chasing them. Suddenly, they saw smoke pouring from one of the bombers after a spitfire had struck its target. The distressed plane dived out across Corfe and the common. With flames engulfing it, it swept across Slepe Farm, hit the trees in Salterns Wood and split up. The engine was later discovered some distance away. The bodies had been flung out and were found hanging in the trees.

This crash can be dated. Rodney Legg records it as 27th September 1940 in his *Battle of Britain Dorset*. The plane was a Messerschmitt Bf.110 and the crewmen were Arthur Niebuhr and Klaus Deissen.

Later, curious spectators seemed to come from everywhere to see the grisly sight. One of them was probably Eddie Anderson, the newspaper boy from Wareham, who recounts that he went searching for the bodies when he came to Arne the following Sunday. In triumph, he took home part of a pilot's boot, with some flesh still clinging to the leather. His mother made him throw it away.

As the farmhouse had the only telephone in the village, the Candys acted as a relay for urgent messages. As soon as the siren went, they used to ring through from Westport House, the Rural District Council Offices at Wareham, or the police station there, and ask someone to alert Keeper Noyce, who was also the local Home Guard organiser. It used to be Phyl who had to go, at all times of the day and night. She got very used to this and confesses that she never used to go to bed in anything other than a pair of slacks and a jumper, just in case. The authorities even provided her with a tin hat for when she had to deliver messages.

Once she did this and nearly got shot! It was at night. The siren went, and so did the telephone, asking her to alert the officer on duty at the camp. She took the back path up the hillside from near the church, and had just reached the fence, when a voice boomed out, "Who goes there?"

"Only me!"

"Who's me?" demanded the sentry, as he began to cock his gun.

"From the farm," Phyl answered in alarm.

The sentry let her through. The moment had passed. She learned later that a new battalion had just taken up duties in the camp, but even today she still remembers that "click-click" of the gun!

Two of the Arne men, Donald Barnes and Reg Smith, were in the local Home Guard unit; No. 2 Platoon, under the command of former Keeper Noyce. Even though he had left Arne and had gone to work for the Bonds, Mr. Noyce was in control of this platoon. Reg rose to the rank of a corporal, and when one of his sergeants was called up, he wanted Reg to take his place. But for the Blitz of 1942, Reg would probably have accepted.

Most of their duty was spent on Harp Hill. In charge of the Ridge platoon was Percy Westerman, the "gungho Boy's Own adventure writer," to quote Rodney Legg. He lived on a houseboat on the River Frome at Wareham, and would often drop over to Arne to check up on them. "We always knew when he was coming. His old English sheep dog'd come in first, so we knew he was about."

Their duty occupied one or two nights a week. Both Donald and Reg were good shots and had the chance to prove their skill when they went on practice in an old clay pit over at Furzebrook. For that, they both got a Red Diamond. Reg had really wanted to join the R.A.F., but when he had gone to register in Wareham, he was told that farming was a reserved occupation, and they would not accept him. When Arne was evacuated in 1942 he tried again, but was again told that in farming he was a keyman.

As the only young person of a highly respected family in the village, Phyl Candy was called on to help out with all kinds of things. Once, she recalls, she was awoken by loud banging on her window sometime during the night. She got up quickly and looked out. Outside were some soldiers from the camp, who told her that a plane had come down and they did not know what had happened to its pilot. They wanted him dead or alive. Would she let them know if she heard anything? On this occasion, she went back to bed and left them to sort it out.

Another time, Major Morris had lost his dog and wanted her help. He had come over from headquarters at Lytchett to visit the camp, and had brought his Alsatian with him. Whilst he was there, the gun had gone off, his dog had bolted in fear. He rang the Candys to ask them to ring camp if they saw the dog. Phyl recalls, "I had the door open. It was a dark night. All of a sudden, something rushed past me, and the dog got under the table. Dad said, "I'm not going to move," so I had to go up to the camp and let them know the dog was down at the farm." They had to wait sometime for the Major to come for his animal, as he had in the meantime gone back to Lytchett.

A frequent visitor who had nothing to do with the army, but whose small efforts were highly regarded at the time was Joyce Burfet, whose father was the chief engineer at Bailey Gate milk factory, near Sturminster Marshall. They kept bees at the back of the schoolhouse, where her father had built an extractor, so Joyce could pour the honey straight into the bottles. Small enterprises like this were very much encouraged during the war, as they were seen to be helping produce more food.

Not all visitors were welcomed. At the beginning of the war, as many refugees escaped from Belgium and later from France, any stranger in the area was regarded with suspicion. There was always the fear that they might be spying. On one occasion, Phyl had been over to Middlebere with some friends, and when she arrived home, her father asked if she had seen any strangers. She told him she had not, but a few minutes later she noticed several people running across the fields. Her father suggested she stayed indoors and ignored them, but she did not.

One of the visitors asked in broken English if they could go inside the church. While they were all safely inside, Phyl rang the police, and then had to keep the strangers in the church until the police arrived. The constables told her they did not know the way down to Russel Quay where the immigrants had a boat, and they asked her to show them the way. "I slipped in to tell mum and dad, and they said I shouldn't go. I said I should be alright," with four soldiers, each with a fixed bayonet! "Two walked with the police in front of me, and two followed." She led this unusual procession down to the quay, where they found the boat and more strangers. Whether they turned out to be innocent refugees fleeing from the continent, or spies, she never did find out.

Another time, she saw from her bedroom window three strangers sitting on the church wall, taking photos when the siren went. She quickly ran up the back path to the camp and told the officer in charge. As they were talking, she could see several people coming across the fields, so she told the guard that she was not going to stop there.

The soldier asked, "What am I supposed to do?"

As he was behind the camp fence and she was outside it, she left his question unanswered and hurried off home. Whether the newcomers were caught, and, if they were, whether they turned out to be refugees, or spies, again she never knew.

But there were spies around, and even the most harmless might have a dangerous mission.

One such was the blind man who lived on a houseboat down at Shipstal. The Candys came to know him quite well. George always gave him a hand up the steps to the church when he wanted to look in, and he used to call in and use their phone quite regularly. Although they were not nosey, Flora and her daughter were fairly puzzled by the references while he was phoning to furniture being moved to Malvern. They could not help but hear his conversations on their phone.

One day in the spring of 1942, the man was passing by the schoolhouse as Phyl was coming out of her front door. She saw him turn and call to her that he wanted to see her. "It occurred to me that if he were blind, he wouldn't be able to see me from that distance."

She reported it, and when the man went into Poole to get his groceries, as he usually did, he was arrested. It turned out that he had been relaying information about the Telecommunications Research Establishment at Worth Matravers, where the R.A.F. had three large radio masts and a mass of radar apparatus. Heading this work was Dr. Robert Cockburn — later knighted — who with his team were trying to find a way of counteracting the radio beam that the Luftwaffe intended to use to direct its bombers against London and other British cities. In May 1942, all was moved to Malvern through fears of a German raid, and hence the spy's references.

Another person who turned out to be a spy was a lady who used to cycle through the village on her way down to Shipstal. She did this journey nearly every week for about a couple of years. Dressed in brown with a brown hat and dark glasses, she gradually became an accepted sight, on her cycle with its little box at the back. Later, the Candys learnt that she too had been arrested as a spy. Her transmitter had been found in a stone quarry near Langton Matravers.

In spite of all this activity that was going on around them, and occasionally above them, the Candy family had their own grief. George, at the age of 82, had had no illness in his life up to Christmas Eve in 1941 when he fell down the five steps into the cellar and had hurt his chest, but apart from this and shock, there was nothing else untoward. On Christmas Day the house was full with visitors, including their married son and daughter, Reg and Vera. Half way through the morning, their father said that he did not think he would be able to eat much as he had a pain in his throat. His family were not too concerned, but when at lunch he could only manage three spoonfuls, they became very worried. Being the festive time, it was difficult to get a doctor, but when one eventually came, George was diagnosed as having cancer of the throat.

For the next few months they fed him on jellies. He struggled on until April when he died. The coffin had to be taken through the upstairs window rather than down the staircase.

Looking back, Phyl supposes that it was fortunate that her father was not alive to experience the Blitz six weeks later. He was spared that night and the trauma that followed which would have killed him.

It was the events of the night of 3rd June 1942 that were to change life in the village completely. On that day, German planes set out to eradicate totally the Royal Naval Cordite Factory at Holton Heath. It was a Wednesday, as Wink Sansom remembers. The German bombers pounded it and returned home with their mission completed, and the area blazing. The following day, Lord Haw-Haw — as William Joyce was dubbed — announced to the world that Holton Heath was burning from one end to the other, with a great loss of life.

What he did not know was that it was not the cordite plant they had hit but the peaceful little backwater of Arne across the other side of the harbour.

This mistake was exactly what the British authorities had hoped and planned for. The loss — or even the crippling — of the Dorset factory would have been disastrous. It was the major source of supply at this time. Only one or two other factories produced cordite and they were much smaller. Holton Heath had to be protected, and the decoy at Arne was deliberately planned.

Opposite Bank Gate cottages, scaffolding had been rigged up to cover pipes carrying the paraffin from the large storage tank. The whole thing gave the impression of a warehouse. Tar barrels cut in half were fixed to the roof. When the Home Guard had orders to set it ablaze, one of the sentries had to go down and turn on the tap letting the paraffin flow along the pipes. Then he had to set light to it, and the whole thing went up like a factory engulfed in flame and led the Luftwaffe away from their real target. It had worked very very well, but at a price, the complete devastation of Arne.

In fact, the destruction could have been even greater. Placed opposite the cottages, the decoy could easily have engulfed them, killing all those who lived there. This possibility the authorities do not seem to have considered.

"The night they got Arne was sheer hell. There were 500-tons of bombs dropped. They absolutely pasted it." recalls Audrey Richards, who then lived with her family over at Furzebrook. "It was one of the worst nights I can ever remember." She was about ten at the time and had just got over pleurisy. Her parents rolled her up in a blanket and carried her down. "We had a cupboard under the stairs where my father put a mattress down for me. We had a dog and cat there, and my father said, 'If anything happens tonight, we are all together.'"

At Ridge, Eva Gover and her family took refuge in their ditch as usual, and at Arne Farm Phyl Candy managed to get her invalid mother down to the cellars, after Headquarters had rung to ask what was happening. Over at

Arne House, the Woods also got down to the cellars. At Bank Gate, Reg and his family had gone to bed as usual.

"About half past twelve, I heard a rat-tat-tat, and the room seemed to be lit up," Reg remembers. It did not take him long to realise what was happening. Dressing quickly, he got his family down into the garden shelter, together with his neighbours, the Diamonds and the Lines.

Then the raid began in earnest, and the villagers knew the full horror of war. Lured by the blazing decoy, the bombs rained down. Phyl reckons that 120 bombs fell that night within a quarter mile radius of the village. In fact, she probably under-estimates the number of bombs that dropped in and around the village. Rodney Legg in *Dorset at War* records the inspection the day afterwards, when Arne decoy was found to be peppered with 206 fresh craters; it was further "estimated that fifty or more bombs also fell into the harbour."

On the night of the attack, the enemy aircraft flew in very very low, so low that fortunately some of the canisters packed with bombs did not do as they were supposed to. They were designed to rotate and come open flinging their deadly contents in all directions. "It would have been fifty times worse if they all had opened," said Jack Spiller, the Fire Chief on duty that night. As it was the whole area was set alight, acres and acres — trees, bracken and heather all burning fiercely.

At Furzebrook, during the raid, Audrey was frightened. "The house seemed to go out and back and cracked right down the front," she still recalls, and a few miles away Reg felt the same; "The bombs were whizzing around. We didn't know if we were up in the air or not in that shelter. It vibrated so."

It was so terrifying, that the lady who lived next door to Reg started praying. "Oh, my good Lord God Almighty. I've never had anything like this in my twenty-eight years like this, O Lord."

Her brother was so worried that he would not stay in the shelter. "It isn't safe in here!" he kept saying.

Reg told him he was a fool if he thought of going outside. "You'll get out there and get hit with shrapnel," but he ignored the advice and went out into the woods until it was all over. "It was frightening when you hear the bombs whizzing down. You didn't know whether it's yours or not!"

Phyl Candy had promised Headquarters to phone them back later, but she never got the chance.The wires were soon brought down, and all contact with the beleaguered village seemed at an end.

John Perks was sent over from Lytchett with his detachment to restore the cables. This was at about 11 o'clock that night. "We couldn't do anything but wait all night, with flames and smoke and darkness (and mosquitoes!) to hinder us."

Reg Smith estimates that they endured two and a half hours of sheer hell during the raid.

The Auxiliary Fire Service from Wareham was despatched in force. Jack Spiller, the local builder of the town, was in the first appliance that managed to get through. By then, the raid had lasted all night. When he first arrived he was forced to stop with his appliance at Bank Gate. It was impossible to get any further. Most of the telegraph wire had come down all across the road. Just then an army officer came past on a motorcycle and asked if there was anything he could do to help. Jack explained that he wanted to get down to the village, at which the officer suggested that if he liked to hop on the back of his machine, he would take him down and his crew could stay at Bank Gate until he returned.

Today, Jack still remembers his nightmare ride with wire snarling around their necks and bringing them off several times. Later, when he had reconnoitred the village, he managed to walk back to where he had left his crew. As he approached it dawned on him that as the hut at the decoy was operated by the Home Guard, they must have a telephone. Jack felt he needed to contact Wareham urgently to get help.

As he drew near, a voice boomed out; "Halt or I'll fire!"

Jack now confesses he was very frightened at this, but managed to call out "I'm the chief of the local fire brigade and I want to get a message back!"

Fortunately, the guard recognised his voice, and introduced himself as Jack Buckley, who knew the fire chief and allowed him to phone for assistance. He asked for twenty appliances, half to be engines and the rest to be mobile dams.

When he did get back to the village again, he found the corner of the Candy's farm on fire. "The iron railings in front of the farm were all twisted in a heap, as if someone had tied knots in them" [Wink Sansom's words]. Jack found Phyl; and her mother still safe in their underground cellar, but the heavy wooden flap-door that covered the steps up into the farmyard had been blown a hundred yards away by the blasts. No doubt mother and daughter were overjoyed to see him, but he was not the first to get through to them. Earlier, at about half past six, soldiers up at the camp had arrived. As they were not sure how many villagers there would be in the cellars, they had brought with them a great bucket of tea! "I took only one mouthful! It was so sweet. I don't take sugar"[Phyl].

Once up and out into the summer morning, they found the house very badly damaged. There were three large holes where shrapnel had sliced through. Upstairs, they found the fireplace in one of the bedroom had been blown onto the bed. A photograph of her sister, which stood on the piano had been twisted round the other way. A vase still stood on the table, but its flowers had totally disappeared! "In a cupboard, we had an old fashioned silver cruet. That was still there, but all the bottles had been blown out. It was most peculiar."

Outside it was heartbreaking to see the havoc one bomb had done to her father's asparagus bed. It had been his pride and joy for about fifty years, and no one else was allowed to touch it. Now it was completely destroyed.

At Slepe Farm, Nancy and her parents were safe behind their retaining wall, although very frightened, "but we kept our fingers crossed," she now recalls.

Over at Furzebrook, Audrey's nextdoor neighbour greeted her family in the morning. "What a bloody awful night we had. Be you alright?" and then old Mr. Newbury of Stoborough, the Air Raid Precautions warden, came over on his bike to see if they were safe.

"When it was all quiet," Reg Smith, his family and neighbours emerged from their shelter, and began to look around them. "Our front door had blown open — blasted open. There was the table all covered in dirt from the bomb blast". He went to inspect the Lines's house. Here the door had also been blown off and the chairs looked as if they had just gone up in the air and down again. The little dog which they had collected from Wareham station the previous day had vanished. They had left him inside the house, but he had escaped when the door blew open. Three days later he was found. "He had gone back to Wareham station, and a porter had picked him up and befriended him," so Mr. and Mrs. Lines got their puppy back.

Safe, too, was Eva in her ditch at Ridge, hearing several army lorries being driven by very very slowly. Her family thought they might be taking the injured to hospital because of their slow speed, but few were injured.

The Woods up at Arne House were also shaken but safe. They were certainly very lucky. An army officer explained to Jack Spiller that they needed to get the Woods out as soon as possible, so Jack called to Mr. Wood to get out, because "you've two unexploded bombs under your house!" They did not need a second warning, and were able to come out through the door from the cellar into the garden that Mr. Wood had built.

When Reg was satisfied that all at Bank Gate were safe, he went off down to Arne. It was a frightening journey, he confesses. Fires were raging on both sides of the road. Trees he had planted as saplings were blazing. Eventually, he did get through and found many cottages were severely damaged. The

Dog Kennels where Keeper Ford lived was battered but still there. The church even showed scars of the night's events, and the cottages at Shipstal had not fared much better.

At Slepe, there was a different problem. Fred Newberry, the Fire Captain, had been touring round trying to ascertain the damage, when Bill Battrick reversed their car and got stuck in a bog. Jess Smith had had to come with a horse and harness and pull the vehicle out.

To help put out the fires at Arne, Wareham summoned crews from all over the south. They even came from as far away as Oxford; twenty machines, which was an unprecedented number for the town.

After they had been on duty for a longtime, one of the army officers came along and asked, "Have you had any food or anything?"

"No, we haven't had anything" came the reply.

"Well," said the officer, "we've still got our kitchen. If you give me half an hour, we'll get something on for you!"

Jack confesses now that "I have never tasted anything so good in all my life," a sentiment that all his crew could utter. They had not had anything for twenty-four hours.

For Dennis Combes, who had witnessed the bombing from the window of the family's house in Nundico in Wareham, it was all very exciting, and, as soon as they could, he and his friends were off down to Arne to collect as many fins from the incendiary bombs as they could find. For them, these were valuable collectors' items.

Because of the great damage to their farmhouse, the Candys could not stay there. Phyl's brother came down and took his mother over to Sturminster Marshall. Phyl herself went to her husband's people at Rollington Farm, near Corfe, until three weeks later that too was taken over by the army, so she went to stay with an aunt in Swanage. A week later, that was hit in a raid!

But to return to the events of the day after the raid; Wink Sansom was attending Wareham market that day, when there was a phone call asking him and Gerald Loxton, the Encombe foreman, who was with him, to go to Arne. "When we arrived, it was a real shambles."

Their first job was to take the Woods and their furniture back to Encombe. It kept them busy for the rest of the day. "We went back for the last load at ten o'clock in the evening, and so we had a drink at the Halfway House. Then off to load up and I got back to Encombe just after midnight. Next morning we were off again."

This time Mr. Loxton said, "We'll have a look in Arne House to see if there's any damage there!"

As the front of the house had been blown out, the damage should have been fairly obvious, but they went to explore nonetheless. "We were just thinking of leaving when an officer told us there was an unexploded bomb there, and I can tell you we were not long in getting out!"

Later, they had to start removing all the farm implements which took them several journeys. "I think we saw enough of Arne to last a lifetime," Wink confesses. "I was sick to death of Arne!"

On the morning after the raid, Reg ran his mum and dad into Wareham in his Ford Eight. "People were talking about the fire. They cheered us up by saying, 'They'll be back again tonight!'"

With this in mind, he and his wife did not go upstairs that night, nor did they want to spend the whole night in the shelter, so they made a bed up for themselves and their son under the dining room table in the front room! The German bombers did not return, though the Smiths did not get much sleep. Fire tenders were working all night long filling up from a pump just outside their door. "It was Bedlam!"

Phyl's Uncle Walter came across to Arne on the day after the raid, and began organising the removal of the Candy's things to the laundry at Encombe. She herself came over several times to get stuff down from the house, but in the short space of time before that happened, the Candys lost things. "A lot was burgled," Phyl surmises. Her mother was accustomed to hang her seal skin cape on an acorn that was carved on the post at the bottom of the stairs. It had once been part of a very long coat, but her sister had shortened it into a cape. It was not found. Only one of the many paintings that were in the house was later found, nor was her father's shaving mug in the shape of a horse and cart, that as a child she had played with for hours on end. That never turned up. Whether they were stolen, or lost in the move, Phyl does not know.

After the things were moved and stored at Encombe, Phyl used to go across to bring

Arne House, where the Woods lived each summer, in ruins at the end of the Second World War.

anything they thought they wanted back to Wareham, where she and her mother had found a place to stay. On one occasion when she went down, there were some Spanish men working on the farm, and she heard them singing. "It sounded so beautiful. [One man] was on top of the hill, and I sat down at the side of the road and waited until he had finished singing. He had a lovely voice."

All the cattle on the Candy's farm had to be destroyed. As a result of the traumatic experience, they had milk fever — all the milk congealed inside them. It was very painful. They all had to be slaughtered.

The fires started during the Blitz continued burning for a long time. Six weeks, according to Reg Smith. Day after day Fred Knight, one of the firemen from Wareham, came down to fight the flames. For over a week, he recalled. The trouble with peat fires is that they will keep breaking out again. The firemen would put the fire out, go away, and the next day or the day after the flames would burst out again. Peat fires, explained Jack Spiller, go in a pincer movement like tanks, and all of a sudden come to a halt when the oxygen is used up. Then when the oxygen roars in, the fire goes off again, "faster than I could run!"

About three weeks after the raid, Headquarters at Weymouth rang up; "Mr. Spiller, there's a fire still in the Arne area. Can you go down and investigate?" So Jack went off, taking an appliance with him. Sure enough he found an area, where the present bird sanctuary is, alight, but during the day time it was difficult to spot. All that could be seen was a mass of white dust over the site, but at night, planes could see it all glowing red. Jack and his men tried again to put it out, but it took them weeks to do this.

Phyl had to drive down to Arne on several occasions to sort out the damaged farmhouse, and on one occasion she remembers flames reaching overhead right across the road. The men in the area advised her to go as quickly as she could through a break in the flames. She knows she was absolutely terrified that the petrol might catch fire. In fact, the terror and the strain of those journeys took its physical toll, and she lost a lot of hair and had to wear it very short. As she recovered, her hair grew again.

It was decided that the whole area had to be evacuated, not just the inhabitants whose houses were damaged. Those living in properties that had not suffered had to leave as well. According to Reg, this was not so much because of the danger from more bombing, but because Churchill and Montgomery and all the big "nobs" who came down to see the damage, looked round and saw the heathland. "What a beautiful place to train troops!" they said.

The two houses at Park, opposite the Dairy House, where the Browns had lived,
derelict at the end of the war.

The scullery at Keeper's Cottage at the end of the war.

As a result, the villagers were given a month's notice to quit. This came as a complete surprise to them, though the Smiths of Slepe Farm had their suspicions when they went into market at Wareham not long after the raid and heard the rumours of this. Nancy recalls her father's comment that the letter would come the next day and it did; a month to get out and sell everything, everything they had built up on the farm during the last nine years; to be out by 10th August. Reg too had an inclination that something was up when Walter Candy wrote to him telling him not to plough up Froxen Point until further notice. Before the Blitz he had been about to prepare this area for the growing of crops. Now he was told to leave it alone.

The National Farmers' Union tried to get a postponement, at least until after the crops were in, to the end of September, but the Army refused, arguing that the Germans would be over before they could harvest their crops. Nancy's father was heartbroken to lose all he worked for and loved, but there was no way round it. Mr. Ron Cottee of Wareham came over to arrange the auction. Job and his wife went over to Nancy's flat at Holton Heath, arranging to put all their own furniture into store. Owen Stevens offered them a farm at Winterborne Zelston, but he would not accept it, arguing that the main road divided the farm in two. He would be worried what might happen if there was an outbreak of foot and mouth disease.

He also refused a farm near Thomas Hardy's birthplace at Bockhampton, saying it had too many watermeadows, and he had had enough of water at Slepe! However, Reg accepted Tom Snow's offer of the 1000-acre farm at Roke, just beyond Bere Regis. Here on chalkland "boy's ground" there was corn in plenty, and that year he put up fifty-one corn ricks. Later when a cottage became vacant, Farmer Snow said he could employ not only his brother, Jess, but also he could give his father part-time work as well.

All the expenses of moving were paid for by Purbeck Rural District Council, and Churchill's van from Wareham took the Smiths and their furniture to Bere. As for the other villagers, some went to the Blandford area.

122

Heath fires are a recurring aspect of Arne life.
This was just one small edge of the great conflagration of 1976.

The Hansfords went over to Okeford Fitzpaine, but what happened to Henry Gardner, Phyl Candy never knew. It was difficult to keep in touch.

From Slepe Cottages, Frank Battrick and his wife, Annie, went to Catseye Cottage on the main road between Corfe and Wareham. This was then two rather tumbled down cottages, certainly not the very well-kept cottage that they have been turned into today. Mrs. Orchard found a home on West Walls in Wareham, and the Govers moved to Ridge.

Dennis Coombes went over to help clear out his grandparents' cottage. He recalls throwing a lot of things out over the garden fence into the rushes. His grandfather's guns went that way. Someone from Poole came over and bought the old man's boat for a pound. The pig was sent for auction, and Dennis had a day off school to see this. The old chap and his wife went over to Organford, to Bere Farm on the Poole road, but he did not last long. "It killed the old man," his grandson said.

For all the villagers the break-up of their community was very, very sad. Life had suddenly come to an end.

The army moved in and the whole area was sealed off to ordinary people. Later, six days before Christmas in 1943, the area was extended and the villagers of Tyneham and Worbarrow were evacuated. Photographs taken at Arne at the end of the war by Monica Hutchings and published in *The Special Smile* show the houses still standing but badly damaged with their stone tiles stripped off in places exposing the rafters. All the windows and doors are missing; not surprising really, since the Army had used the village for training, where they could simulate the capture of an enemy held French village and practice house-to-house fighting.

At the Browns' cottage, the men ripped out all the banisters and used them for firewood. Over at Slepe, it was the navy that used the area for training, their shells ripping holes through what was a new building.

In the months leading up to D-Day, the peninsula became the home of hundreds of American soldiers, again for battle practice, preparation for the reconquest of France. The First, Second, Fourth, Ninth, Twenty-eighth, Twenty-ninth, Thirtieth, and the Ninetieth Infantry Divisions of the United States Army that went to Normandy, but so far it has been impossible to trace any survivors who remember training in this area of the Isle of Purbeck. "You didn't know what was going on down there [at Arne] after the army took over." At Ridge, Joan Green "saw despatch riders going up and down" the road to Arne.

The Yanks, Eva Gover recalled, were billeted amongst other places all along the other side of the hedge opposite her house. Every day when they looked out they saw them and heard their guns booming out. "Everything jumped off the mantlepiece every time they fired." But gradually they got used to it, even if Eva's baby brother did not. He was frightened to death when he head the noise, so she used to say; "The man put the shell in the gun, and the gun went bang!" She tried to make this coincide with the explosion, but it did not seem to go any good. He still screamed. "The weird thing was there was always activity up and down the road, and for us kids who lived in the country it was just total hell, being used to quiet!"

There were other experiences for them. It was the first time they had seen a coloured person, other than on the cinema screen. The Richards family at Furzebrook could agree with this. One day as she was on her way home from Stoborough School with her friends, young Audrey had a bad attack of asthma, and collapsed on the ground. Her friends did not know what to do, but a lorry pulled up and an American voice enquired; "What's the matter with the kid?"

When the friends told him about the attack, the yank asked "Where does she live?"

Audrey was aware of a big black American gently picking her up and cradling her in his arms, carrying her indoors. He came back the next day to see how she was, and came back several more days as well.

Then, suddenly, all the activity stopped, the men, guns and everything had disappeared in the night, and there was nothing but silence. "We got up one morning and they were all, gone. It was very weird. All this noise and activity and all those thousands of men going up and down the road, and one morning it was all, gone." Later, of course, the news went out that Allied troops had landed in Normandy.

This was 6th June 1944 — D-Day.

Sources
Eva Biles; Nina Bishop; Dorrie Churchill; Gladys Clark; Dennis Coombes; Joan Jacobs; Fred Knight; Phyl Marsh; Audrey Richards; Wink Sansom; Jack Spiller; Reg Smith, and Nancy Strowbridge.
Jim Hearmon; Ron Kiddle; Don Gilbert, all former soldiers at Arne. Fred George and Roy Lane, both ex-Army.
Rodney Legg, *Battle of Britain Dorset*, 1995.
  Dorset Aviation Encyclopaedia, 1996.
  Dorset at War, 1986.
  Literary Dorset, 1990.
  Swanage Encyclopaedic Guide, 1995.
John Perks, *Dorset's A. A. Defences*, 1993.

Landing craft moored in the Wareham Channel, off Russel Quay, after President de Gaulle pulled France out of Nato during the Cold War.

IX
Back to Nature

Arne was completely altered by the Blitz and the exodus of its inhabitants, as were nearby Povington and the more well known Tyneham on the other side of the Purbeck Hills. Unlike these two places, Arne's villagers were allowed back after the war, but few came. Many had died because of having to move, and those that could come back had put down roots elsewhere and did not want another upheaval.

After three years of being a battle training ground for troops, all of the cottages were in ruins. When John Perks visited the area sometime before D-Day, he found most of the houses very badly damaged. After the war, some could be repaired — the schoolhouse, the dairy, the keeper's cottage, those at Bank Gate, and Arne House were all patched up and made inhabitable.

Froxen Copse seen before the mining of clay on the Gold Point peninsula.

Many were too far gone and had to be pulled down.The Browns' at Park, the cottages at Slepe and at Shipstal, and the Candys' farm, all went. What was left of the latter, Arne Farm, survived until 1954, when it was pulled down and the rubble taken away. A new farmhouse went up, but further back, and nearer to where Henry Gardner's cottage had stood.

At Slepe, Reg and Nancy's parents had been promised that after the war they would be allowed back, but in the meantime their father had died, so it was only their mother and three brothers who returned to a derelict farm. First the ploughing had to be done, and then the farm repaired.

To the Dairy House came a newcomer, Colonel Eric Scott. He was new only in the sense he had not lived here before, but since he was one of the Scotts of Encombe he would have been familiar with Arne before the war. He began pig-breeding, starting with two pigs. Gradually, he built up a herd of seventy-five sows, Saddlebacks crossed with a white boar. He had to build his own pig-hut, which he did from an old Anderson shelter with its walls flattened out and sheets placed over the top. He seems to have done quite well here.

Just before he arrived, John Crichton and his wife, Judith, came in the autumn of 1950 and began setting up a dairy herd, concentrating on milk production.

About the same time, Dr. Graham Humby and his family had moved into Arne House. He had been an air-pilot and also one of those plastic surgeons who became very important rebuilding badly damaged faces of pilots. The estate would not grant him a lease on the House as there was no money to repair it, but he moved in in any case, and pulled a tarpaulin up over the holes in the roof. There he lived for a time, introducing Welsh black sheep, and keeping cattle [Galloway and Hereford crossbreeds]. He tried experimenting with the idea of harvesting spartina grass and turning it into cattle-feed, but little came of it.

So the village gradually began to come alive again, but apart from the Smiths it was with new people. Obviously there are no villages in the country which have not changed since 1939. All have changed, new people, and new houses. The popularity of the motorcar from the 1950s onwards has brought strangers to live in the countryside, but often to work and shop in neighbouring towns. Together with the great increase in the country's population, this has resulted in large housing estates being built to accommodate the arrivals. In some villages, these now are larger than the old village, and the newcomers swamp those whose roots are there. Even the older houses have been, in some cases, drastically altered. From the 1950s through to the 1980s it was the fashion to get rid of the old and put up something modern, often completely out of keeping with the character of the village. Shops have been altered too, and the village school may well have closed.

During the half century after the war, every place changed, but the changes have been gradual, often piecemeal, even imperceptible until they happened. For Arne, the change was swift. A sudden break with the past in 1942 when the inhabitants were forced out, and when after 1945 they were allowed back, it was largely with new people, beginning a new life, restoring bomb-damaged houses, or completely rebuilding them.

With less people coming to live here, there has come another change which makes the village most unusual. Nature has been allowed to take over vast areas.

In 1954, the Nature Conservancy designated the Big Wood here — just nine acres but in a remarkable strip of changing vegetation from salt-marsh through to trees — as a National Nature Reserve, and later the Royal Society for the Protection of Birds acquired a further 916 acres as a bird sanctuary. These two areas were supplemented in 1982, when the National Trust was given, as part of the Bankes estate, Hartland Moor and the Middlebere

One of the largest of its properties, the R.S.P.B. reserve at Arne was established to protect the main nesting area of the Dartford Warbler.
The area has since been extended. Current boundaries are shown on the map, on page 5.

peninsula, to the south and east of Arne. "The best bog in Dorset," was how Rodney Legg described the moor in his *National Trust Dorset*, "Purbeck's giant sponge, an acid bog" whose colour changes during the seasons from rosy-purple to brilliant blue as the plant life it supports flower. "The importance of the Bankes estate passing into the National Trust ownership," he continued, "is that it safeguards a magnificent jumble of wild and marginal lands."

Thus, in a sense the whole of Arne and its environs have been set aside as an area of outstanding scientific importance, and therefore the assumption was that its countryside would be preserved and spared the caravans, housing estates, second homes, and such like, that seem to go with tourist development, and this had happened.

But the preservation has been achieved only after a series of battles with English China Clays who wish to exploit the area's valuable minerals. The type of clay found here is ball clay, an essential ingredient in pottery making, which manufacturers have been using ever since the eighteenth century, though it was not taken very much from this area in the nineteenth century. ECC acquired the mineral rights here as long ago as 1950, but they did not seek to use them until the 1970s, when they wanted to open a large pit at Froxen Copse, "an attractive belt of old woodland" [Legg], on the extreme northern side of the peninsula.

As a result a huge emotional outcry resounded from ecologists and conservationists alike arguing that mining would destroy the unique lowland heath, and with it the habitat that supports a whole range of threatened life. Among them was the Dartford Warbler, one of Britain's rarest breeding birds, which nests principally in the peninsula.

When in 1977, the Environment Secretary, Peter Shore, upheld the rights of the mining company, conservation groups were furious.

Dr. Michael Gane of the Nature Conservancy condemned the decision as a "setback for nature concern in southern England." "A retrograde step," declared the British Trust for Ornithology. "Disastrous," wrote M. J. Everett in the magazine British Birds.

Yet, in spite of this widespread criticism, the visitor today might well ask what all the fuss was about. These battles and the subsequent victory for exploitation do not appear to be so disastrous. They will look at the achievements of the R.S.P.B., its nature trails and the peace and solitude here. The extraction of the ball clay cannot be seen in the village, and the mining company have been very discrete about the extraction. For most people, nature seems to have quietly taken over.

Thus, Arne, like every other place, is not the same as it was in the 1930s. It cannot be. Life goes on, and symbolic of this is the church. The medieval building is still here. Its battle scars restored. It has become a magnet for architectural lovers and those who welcome the rhythms of the old prayer book. The Bishop of Salisbury reopened it in an important service of Rededication, but today taking the service might well be the Reverend Margaret Mauraine, who as a priest from Wareham is one of those new vicars!

Arne has moved with the times and, ironically, back to nature!

Sources
Bournemouth Evening Echo, undated newspaper cutting, about 1953.
Western Gazette, undated newspaper cutting, about 1953.
Rodney Legg, *National Trust Dorset*, 1987.
　　　　Purbeck Island, revised edition, 1989.
Eric Scott; Judith Crichton; and Reg Smith.

Conservation grazing resplendent on Stoborough Heath National Nature Reserve,
in the shape of an English Long Horn Cross
(don't tell anyone, but No 109 prefers heather to grass).

*Blasted heath as it was left after drought-time fires and arson which devastated
Purbeck's National Nature Reserves in 1976.*

Lowland bog, at Hartland Moor National Nature Reserve, seen from Slepe.

Sources Consulted

1. Published Sources
A Descriptive Account of Southampton — Illustrated, c.1892-98.
Reverend John Hutchins, *The History and Antiquities of the County of Dorset*, 2nd edition, 808; 4th edition, ed. W. Shipp and J. Hodson, vol. 1, 1861, reprinted 1973. Royal Commission on Historical Monuments, *An Inventory of Historical Monuments in the County of Dorset*, vol.2, The South-East, Part 1, 1970.

2. Published Sources; Newspapers and Directories
Burke's Peerage, 1931.
Kelly and Co. *Post Office Directory for Hants, Wilts., and Dorset*, 1848; 1855; 1859; 1867; 1880.
Post Office Directory of Dorset 1885; 1890; 1898; 1903; 1911; 1915; 1927; 1931; 1935; and 1939.
Bournemouth Evening Echo, 26th Oct. 1907; 29th Dec. 1974; 9th May 1991.
Western Gazette, 9th May 1947.
Who's Who, 1945.

3. Unpublished Sources
Memoirs of Wink Sansom.
Arne;   Churchwardens' Accounts, D.C.R.O., PE/ARN.
          Parish Registers, D.C.R.O. PE/ARN.
          School Logbooks, D.C.R.O.
          Tithe Map and Plan, 1847 D.C.R.O., D PIT/P1.
          Census Returns 1841; 1851; 1861; 1871; and 1891. D.C.R.O.

4. Secondary Sources; Published
M. Bowditch, *Cordite — Poole*, undated.
A. Fagersten, *The Place-Names of Dorset*, 1933.
Barbara Kerr, *Bound To The Soil*, 1968.
Rodney Legg, *Battle of Britain Dorset*, 1995.
          Dorset at War, 1986.
          Dorset Aviation Encyclopaedia, 1996.
          Literary Dorset, 1990.
          National Trust Dorset, 1987.
          Purbeck Island, revised edition, 1989.
          Swanage Encyclopaedic Guide, 1993.
A. D. Mills, *The Place Names of Dorset*, vol. 1., 1977.
National Environment Research Council, *Poole Harbour*, 1985.
John Perks, *Dorset's A. A. Defences*, 1990.

5. Oral Sources
Eddie Anderson; Eva Biles (nee Gover); Nina Bishop; Eddie Blow; Dorothy Churchill (nee Brown); Gladys Clark (nee Brown); Harry Clarke; Dennis Coombes; Florence Coombes (nee Battrick); Sheilah Cooper; Roy Dean; Bob Dorey; Hugh Elmes; Jack Fancy; Neil Gartshore, Warden at Arne, RSBP Nature Reserve; F. George; Don Gilbert; James Grasby, Assistant Historic Buildings Officer for Wessex; Brian Hallett; J. J. Hearmon; George Holland; Joan Jacobs (nee Green); Ron Kiddle; Roy Lane; Phyl Marsh (nee Candy); Tom Newberry; Betty Pettey; Dennis Proudley; Audrey Richards; Will "Wink" Sansom; Colonel E. S. Scott; Reginald Smith; Jack Spiller; Frank Strowbridge; Nancy Strowbridge (nee Smith); Joan Sturdy (nee Wood); and Fred Zimmerman.

6. Miscellaneous Sources
The County Archivist and staff of the Dorset County Record Office; The Enquiries Staff at the University of Keele, Staffordshire; The staff at Manchester Central Reference Library; The staff at Poole Reference Library; The staff of the Hamphire County Council Library Department in Southampton; George Large, Archivist, Royal Institute of Painters in Water Colours; A. W. Potter, Research Assistant at the Royal Academy of Arts; Brigadier K. A. Timbers, Historical Secretary of The Royal Artillery Historic Trust; Major J. D. Braisley, R.A. (Retd.), Editor of *Gunner*; and Sarah Duffield, National Society Archivist.

7. Photographic Material
The author is grateful to all those who loaned the photographs used. Most have come from the various families mentioned in the text; historic prints from the Rodney Legg collection; and late twentieth century photographs from the Dorset Publishing Company archive. Copies of the latter are available from the publishers.

Index